****

Forward-

****

My friend, Roger Boguski, has written on a tough subject, "THE CROWN JEWEL OF THE OLDER TESTAMENT," but he has done so with passion and style. Roger has served as a Pastor for 20 years and as a Jewish missionary since 2000, and has a unique understanding of this chapter. His insight into chapter 53 of Isaiah will create in you a deep love for Jesus like never before. This is one chapter in the scriptures that is necessary, not only to read but to understand. The details of this event are in the scriptures but cannot be understood fully with a layman's eye. Roger sees what we could never see. I highly recommend that every serious follower of Jesus Christ read and digest this study.

    Harold Michael Phillips, PhD
    Senior Pastor Pleasant View Baptist Church
    Port Deposit, MD

    Author, "God's Leadership Codes:" A Biblical Look at Moses' Leadership Training Before God!

****

Preface-

****

Isaiah 53 has been called the forbidden chapter. Why? The Rabbis do not include this chapter in the Haftarah readings in the synagogue. Why? There is confusion about the meaning of this chapter in the Jewish community. Why? The answer is quite simple. Because Isaiah 53, known as the crown jewel of the older testament, points directly to Jesus, the Anointed one, the Messiah, as the suffering servant. The prophet Isaiah prophesied about 700 years before Jesus was born that the Messiah would be rejected by his people, and that he would suffer horribly and die to make atonement for the sins of the world. This Messiah is Jesus, the Son of God, who came in the flesh to save humanity as the newer testament testifies.

Reverend Roger T. Boguski, whom I have known for fifty years and affectionately known as Pastor B, has been sharing the gospel with Jewish people for over five decades. Over the years, he has been teaching others the Bible and how to talk to their Jewish friends. Besides his study of the Scriptures, he studied under Rabbi's teachings to better understand how to reach Jewish people with the Good News. He loves the Jewish people and desires for them to know the Messiah. He is more than qualified to write on Isaiah 53 with his years of ministry to Jewish people and study of this passage. This book is the culmination of a lifetime's work.

This book will be a blessing to you as you appreciate The Crown Jewel of the Older Testament even more. You will reflect anew on the suffering Servant and His sacrifice, and marvel once again at our Savior, Jesus.

Dr. Russell S. Woodbridge

Contents

Forward

Preface

The Prophet Isaiah

Who is the Servant in Isaiah?

Chapter One: The Servant Exalted, Isaiah 52:13-15
   Part One: The Servant's Triumphal Entry – Isa. 52:13
   Part Two: The Servant's Terrifying Exit – Isa. 52:14
   Part Three: The Servant's Tremendous Eulogy – Isa. 52:15

Chapter Two: The Servant Despised, Isaiah 53:1-3
   Part One: The Servant's Arm Nurtured – Isa. 53:1
   Part Two: The Servant's Roots Matured – Isa. 53:2
   Part Three: The Servant's Sorrow Unveiled – Isa. 53:3

Chapter Three: The Servant Wounded, Isaiah 53:4-6
   Part One: The Servant Afflicted Mercilessly – Isa. 53:4
   Part Two: The Servant Wounded Fatally – Isa. 53:5
   Part Three: The Servant Stricken Internally – Isa. 53:6

Chapter Four: The Servant Cut-off, Isaiah 53:7-9
   Part One: The Servant's Illicit Arrest – Isa. 53:7
   Part Two: The Servant's Illegal Trial – Isa. 53:8
   Part Three: The Servant's Illogical Burial – Isa. 53:9

Chapter Five: The Servant Satisfied, Isaiah 53:10-12
   Part One: The Servant's Soul Suffers – Isa. 53:10
   Part Two: The Servant's Soul Satisfies – Isa. 53:11
   Part Three: The Servant's Soul Supplicates – Isa. 53:12

Ancient Rabbinic Thoughts

Endnotes

Bibliography

The Prophet Isaiah

"The vision of Isaiah, **the son of Amoz**, which he saw concerning Judah and Jerusalem in the days of Uzziah, Jotham, Ahaz and Hezekiah, kings of Judah." Isaiah 1:1. His call to service is unrecorded, but in chapter six we have his vision and commitment. The word vision is the word (*chazone*) and is a direct revelation or message from God. Where there is no vision the people perish, Prov. 29:18 (*para*) run wild, are unkempt, unrestrained, out of control; Why? They take the lead, doing what's right in their own eyes, promoting wickedness, uncovering themselves, going naked! Like the golden calf experience in Exodus 33. Where there is no vision the people perish, but where there is no commitment the world will go to Hell!

Twelve times in the Older Testament, Isaiah is introduced as, "the son of Amoz." Not the prophet Amos, who was a shepherd and a fig-picker but Amoz (the strong one) who according to Jewish tradition was the brother of Amaziah, King of Judah and the father of King Uzziah, which would have made Isaiah and Uzziah cousins. However, whoever he was, he was well known by the readers of the Older Testament, of that day because just mentioning his son was all the introduction Isaiah needed. In the book of Isaiah we find the form of his name as **Yesha'yahu** meaning, 'Salvation is of Yahweh' or 'Yahweh is Salvation,' a name which to an extent epitomizes the message of Isaiah. His name is obviously significant but it is never explained nor elaborated on in Scripture.

He was clearly raised in a well to do family and received a very good education. H.C. Leupold comments on Isaiah saying, "Hardly anyone would question the claim that Isaiah is a prince among prophets. His eloquence is very evident, he has at his command a vocabulary richer than that of any prophet, even more comprehensive than that of the book of Psalms." He was not a sheepherder like Amos or a priest like Ezekiel, but he was a prophet of kings and a prince among the prophets. His preaching on 'personal holiness' did not come without a price-tag however, the same as it does in today's pulpits. The price of personal holiness is, 'personal loneliness!' Any preacher who starts preaching on holiness today will be a very lonely man, many times even in his own home.

Isaiah made his home in Jerusalem and his home was a godly one. His wife was one of the four women referred to in the Scriptures as a prophetess in, Isa. 8:3. His two sons were named prophetically; *'Shear-Jashub'* (a remnant shall return) a pledge referring to the nation of Judah if captured, would always return to Jerusalem and would never become extinct, even today! After 2,500 years they are back in their ancient land, speaking their ancient language and they did it on the very day the Ancient of Days gave them, "The Sabbath!" Also, *'Maher-Shalal-Hash-Baz'* means (haste to the spoil; haste to the prey; swift to the booty) a prophecy that the Assyrians would ravage and subdue the land or soon plunder the kingdom of Judea. Often names were given for signs and wonders in Israel. Many still name their children Isaiah today, but none name their children *Shear-Jashub* or *Maher-Shalal-Hash-Baz*.

Isaiah lived around 100 years and ministered for about 60-70 years. The testimony of the Jewish people, the Talmud, tradition, and the early Church Fathers along with several other sources say that, wicked king Manasseh had Isaiah stuffed into a hollow log and sawed in two at the pool of Siloam, with a wood saw. (ouch!) Even, Hebrews 11:37 speaks of those, "That were stoned, that were sawn asunder..." Many believe this could be a reference to Isaiah.

The Evidence seems to be in Favor of Isaiah writing this book, in fact the book of Isaiah has been called the 'Fifth Gospel' because of its emphasis on salvation, the coming Messiah, and the 'Suffering Servant.' For centuries Isaiah has been known as the 'Old Testament Evangelist.' His prophecies were described as, 'The Gospel According to Isaiah.' There are over 333 predictive, precise prophecies concerning the first coming of Israel's Messiah; some scholars say, there are over 456. The Newer Testament presents the Messiah in **'All of His fullness,'** whereas Isaiah presents, **'The fullness of the Messiah.'** Isaiah is quoted over 100 times in the Newer Testament, more than all the other Older Testament prophets combined.

One of the problems people have today with the book of Isaiah is authorship due to, 'Higher Criticism' which rejects the Bible as being historically accurate because they don't believe the Scriptures contain, 'Predictive Prophecy.' In essence they deny super-naturalism and a favorite target of theirs is the book of Isaiah. They believe the book of Isaiah was written by two or even three authors over several hundred years with several editors who lived in different time periods. The belief that one man, the son of Amoz, in the 8th century BCE was inspired by God and wrote the whole book and predicted events and people hundreds of years before they occurred is preposterous and a dishonest presentation. That's true, only if you do not believe in the doctrine of verbal, plenary inspiration and precise, predictive prophecy. In other words they don't believe in an omnipotent, omnipresent, omniscient, omnificent, God!

The higher critics divide Isaiah into three parts Trito-Isaiah, chapters 1-39 written by Isaiah; chapters 40-55 written by another person after the Babylonian captivity; and chapters 56-66 written by yet another person sometime around the time of Christ. Most hold to a two-fold view of Isaiah or what is called 'Deutero-Isaiah' dividing it between chapters 1-39 and 40-66 for the same reasons. The higher critics reject Isaiah because he predicts the future in many places and yet many of those predictions have already been fulfilled. However, the critics don't present a scientific study of the Bible or prophecy. They just assume super-naturalism is impossible!

There is no indication that the Septuagint LXX, a Greek translation of the Older Testament dated around 250 BCE, sees any part of the book of Isaiah being written over a period of time. Also, in the 'Dead Sea Isaiah Scroll' which contains all 66 chapters of Isaiah, there is no division between chapters 39 and 40. In fact chapter 40 begins on the same scroll and on the same column as chapter 39. Also ancient Rabbinic Jewish tradition never once mentions two or three authors for Isaiah. Another evidence of the book's unity is the common themes or topics that flow throughout the entire book, these pose a real problem for the higher critics. Then you have phrases like, "Holy One of Israel" used 25 times in Isaiah, 12 times in chapters 1-39, 11 times in chapters 40-55, and 2 times in chapters 56-66, this consistency lends itself to the conclusion that one author wrote one harmonious book.

The strongest theological reason for accepting the unity and the reliability of Isaiah as the one and only author of the book of Isaiah is that the Newer Testament declares it to be so. In John 12:38-41, John the apostle put together Isaiah 53:1 and Isaiah 6:9-10 citing both as from the same Isaiah not two. He stated, "That the saying of Isaiah, the prophet, might be fulfilled, which he spoke, Lord, who hath believed our report? And to whom hath the arm of the Lord been revealed? Therefore, they could not believe, because that Isaiah said again, He hath blinded their eyes, and hardened their heart; that they should not see with their eyes, nor understand with their heart, and be converted, and I should heal them. These things said Isaiah, when he saw his glory, and spoke of him."

In fact *Yeshua/Jesus* Himself read from Isaiah 61:1-2, a section the higher critics deny Isaiah wrote in Luke 4:17-21, and He never said anything to the contrary. Both John and Jesus saw the passages as predictions of Isaiah so we can be assured of the divinely provided unity and the historical reliability of the book of Isaiah. "God said it, and I believe it, so that settles it, for me!" How about you? Do you need more evidence?

There is more, Ecclesiasticus 48:22-25; Josephus, Antiquities 11:1-2; Literary style and more repetitious words; Internal evidence matching Isaiah 40-66 with the Newer Testament; Matt. 3:3; 12:17-21; Luke 3:3-6; Acts 8:28; Romans 10:16, 20. The same phrase, "The mouth of the LORD has spoken it," repeated in, Isaiah 1:20; 40:5; 58:14, in all three divisions. *"The vision of Isaiah, the son of Amoz, which he saw concerning Judah and Jerusalem in the days of Uzziah, Jotham, Ahaz, and Hezekiah, kings of Judah."* Isaiah 1:1.

We will be discussing the prophecy of Isaiah, the son of Amoz, in chapter 52:13 - 53:12 in detail. So, it's important for you to stay with me but it's not important for you to remember or even understand every detail I am saying. What is important though is, "What you think, as a result of what I am about to say!" Now that is very important!

****

Who Is The Servant In Isaiah?

Before we can properly examine the 'Crown Jewel' of the prophet Isaiah, we must identify the '<u>Servant</u>' Isaiah is referring to in chapter 52:13 – 53:12. Modern Jewish writers would lead us to believe it is Israel and modern Christian writers would lead us to believe it is Israel's Messiah. The word '<u>Servant</u>' is found 23 times in Isaiah and it is the Hebrew word (*eh-bed*) for servant, attendant, indentured or owned servant. In 'Paleo-Hebrew' or ancient Hebrew before the Babylonian captivity, the three Hebrew letters that make up the root of this word are (*ayin-bet-dalet*) and form a pictogram, "To see/experience - your household/family - through the front door." This indentured '<u>Servant</u>' was part of the family and had access and privileges to the family by the front door <u>not</u> the back door. This is a servant of privilege, status and rank and he has the privilege to enter the home like a son would and he sees everything.

A Survey of the word '<u>Servant</u>' shows us that this word appears 23 times in the book of Isaiah and it would be to our advantage to do a quick survey of those 23 occurrences. The first time the word '<u>Servant</u>' appears, it is referring to the author Isaiah himself in Isaiah 20:3, "And the LORD said, As **My <u>servant</u> Isaiah**, has walked naked and barefoot three years for a sign and a wonder upon Egypt and upon Ethiopia;" As a sign against Egypt and Ethiopia.

The next occurrence is in Isa. 22:20 when God replaces Shebna with Eliakim, "And it shall come to pass in that day, that I will call **My <u>servant</u>, Eliakim**, the son of Hilkiah;" Then you have the word servant used in Isaiah 24:2 in a comparison of terms; the people with the priest; **the <u>servant</u> with the master**; the maid with her mistress; the buyer with the seller, etc. Then you have a reference to King David as the servant in Isaiah 37:35, "For I will defend this city to save it for Mine own sake, and for **My <u>servant</u> David's** sake."

Next, Israel is named as the servant in Isaiah 41:8-9, "**But thou Israel, art My <u>servant</u>**, Jacob whom I have chosen, the seed of Abraham My friend; Thou, whom I have taken from the ends of the earth, and called thee from the chief men thereof, and said unto thee, **Thou art My <u>servant</u>**; I have chosen thee, and not cast thee away."

The next time we find the word 'Servant' is in Isaiah 42:1-4, "**Behold My <u>servant</u>**, whom I uphold; Mine elect, in whom My soul delights; I have put My Spirit upon him; he shall bring forth judgment to the Gentiles. He shall not cry, nor lift up, nor cause his voice to be heard in the street. A bruised reed shall he not break, and the smoking flax shall he not quench; he shall bring forth judgment in truth. He shall not fail nor be discouraged, till he have set judgment in the earth; and the isles shall wait for his law." There is a twofold account of this servant, first as a weak, despised, rejected, and slain <u>servant</u> and then as a mighty conqueror taking vengeance on the nations and restoring Israel.

To resolve this problem Rabbis adopted the theory of two Messiahs, 'Messiah ben Joseph' the suffering Messiah who dies in a battle against Edom/Rome; Followed by 'Messiah ben David' the triumphant messiah who establishes his Kingdom of righteousness after defeating the Gentile nations. Another attempt to deal with this seeming contradiction is mentioned in *Pesikta Rabbathi*, (Jewish Commentary) where Messiah ben David suffers in every generation for every generation's sins.

Many Rabbis are just awaiting the coming of Elijah who will make all things clear. One thing is clear however, Isa. 42:1 is not referring to Israel as the <u>servant</u>, that's for sure because as chapter 42 goes on we see Israel chosen, sinning and chastened and then in chapter 43, redeemed and restored by the '<u>Servant</u>' in 42:1. Also this is not referring to Israel because it is quoted in the Newer Testament in Matthew 12:14-21 as referring to *Yeshua/Jesus* in total.

As was just seen in Isaiah 42:8ff the nation of Israel is in focus, chosen, sinning and chastened; so in 42:19 the servant is obviously Israel, "Who is blind, but **My servant?** Or deaf as My messenger that I sent? Who is blind as he that is perfect, and blind as **the LORD's servant**?" We see this question answered in v. 22-24 and then in chapter 43 we see Israel is to be redeemed and restored and to be not only His servant but His witnesses, "Ye are My witnesses, saith the LORD, and **My servant** whom I have chosen, that you may know and believe Me, and understand that I am He;

before Me there was no God formed, neither shall there be after me. I, even I am the LORD, and beside Me there is no Savior." Isa. 43:10-11.

Isaiah Chapter 44 is chuck full of promises to Israel, in 44:1-2, the servant is definitely Israel, "Yet now hear, **O Jacob, My servant**, and Israel whom I have chosen. Thus saith the LORD that made thee from the womb, who will help thee; Fear not, **O Jacob, My servant**, and thou, Jeshurun, whom I have chosen." (Jeshurun is a poetical name for Israel). He promises to pour out His Spirit upon their seed and His blessings upon their offspring and then in vv. 21-27 He promises to forgive their sins and return them to their land, "Remember these, O Jacob and Israel; **for thou art My servant**; I have formed thee, **thou art My servant, O Israel**, thou shalt not be forgotten by Me. I have blotted out like a thick cloud thy transgressions and like a cloud thy sins; return unto Me, for I have redeemed thee."

There is no doubt this servant is Israel, however in v. 26 after much study I believe, the servant is either Isaiah or God's prophets; "Who confirms the word of **His servant,** and performs the counsel of His messengers; "Again Israel is reminded of God's promises to them in chapter 48:20, the servant is identified as Israel, "Go forth from Babylon, flee from the Chaldeans; with a voice of singing declare, tell this, utter it even to the end of the earth; say: The LORD has redeemed **His servant Jacob**."

Now, starting in Isaiah 49-57 we have what is referred to as the **"Suffering Servant Section"** of Isaiah and it starts off with Israel being identified as the servant in v.3, "And said unto me, **Thou art my servant, O Israel,** in whom I will be glorified." Because of this verse Rashi an 11th century, non-Messianic, French Jewish scholar, whose initials (Rashi) stand for *Rabbi Shlomo Itzhaki* said, that the servant in Isaiah 53 is Israel. By the way Rashi lived between the first and second crusades and his stand was a reaction to Christian scholars who proposed that Isaiah chapter 53 was a fulfillment of *Yeshua/Jesus*. Then Joseph Kimchi and his son David in 1105-1235 followed Rashi as did Don Isaac Abarbanel of Spain in 1437-1508.

However, Isaiah 49:5 takes on a different Servant tone. "And now, saith the LORD who formed me from the womb **to be His servant**, to bring Jacob again to Him, Though Israel be not gathered, yet shall I be glorious in the eyes of the LORD, and my God shall be my strength."

Obviously **this servant** is not Israel because **this servant** is going to bring Jacob/Israel to the LORD, even though Israel is not gathered, **this servant** shall be glorious in the eyes of the LORD. Also v.6 goes on to **embellish this servant,** "And he said, It is a light thing that thou should be *my servant* to raise up the tribes of *Jacob,* and to restore the preserved of Israel; I will also give thee for a light to the Gentiles, that thou may be my salvation *(yeshua)* unto the end of the earth." How could Israel raise up Israel and restore Israel and be a light to the Gentiles and salvation to all mankind?

They simply are not, have not, and will not be doing that until the time of 'Jacob's Trouble' known as the 'Great Tribulation' when 144,000 male, virgin, Jewish, men from the twelve tribes of Israel will be commissioned to do exactly that! Rev. 7&14. So, Israel cannot be the servant in v.5 and v.6. How about v.7, "Thus saith the LORD, the Redeemer of Israel, and His Holy One, to Him whom man despiseth, *to him whom the nation abhorreth*, **to a servant of rulers**: Kings shall see and arise, princes shall worship, because of the LORD who is faithful, and the Holy One of Israel, and he shall choose thee." This servant can't be Israel if Israel as a nation is going to abhor this servant!

In Isaiah 50 we see the humiliation of the '<u>Servant,</u>' in v.6, "I gave my back to the smiters, and my cheeks to them that plucked off the hair, I hid not my face from shame and spitting. For the Lord GOD will help me; therefore shall I not be confounded; therefore have I set my face like a flint, and I know that I shall not be ashamed." This is not Israel, this is a person who has been beaten, had his beard ripped out, been spit upon, humiliated, and disgraced: Then v.10 says, "Who is among you that fears the LORD, that **obeys the voice of His <u>servant</u>**, that walks in darkness, and has no light? Let him trust in the name of the LORD, and stay upon his God." The LORD is asking Israel a question, who among them fears the LORD, obeys the servant's voice, walks in darkness, etc. If Israel is the servant then how can they answer these questions or even obey the servant's voice?

Then we come to Isaiah 52:13, **"Behold My Servant!"** Again he is not identified, but we shall see that he is made a sin offering and here he is *exalted, extolled and elevated.* Three words lifting him higher and higher and higher, the only other time these three words are used together in

Scripture are in Isaiah 30:10 and they are used of the LORD, "Now will I **rise**, saith the LORD, now will I be **exalted**, now will I **lift up** Myself."

Another incident that comes close to this is in Isa. 6:1, "In the year that King Uzziah died, I saw also the LORD sitting on a throne, **high and lifted up**, and His train filled the temple." If these words are applied to the LORD, the *YHWH*, then this servant must be on an equal plane with the LORD, Jehovah.

Then the final servant passage is in Isaiah 53:11, "He shall see the travail of his soul, and shall be satisfied *(saba)*; by his knowledge shall **my righteous <u>servant</u>** justify many; for he shall bear their iniquities." Behold My servant exalted, extolled, elevated; My righteous servant, how on earth can this refer to any group of people no matter how honorable we think they might be? My own grandmother is not worthy of this accolade.

Read chapter one of Isaiah for a graphic description of Israel and then tell me if they fit into Isaiah 52:13 and 53:11. "I have nourished and brought up children and they have rebelled against Me. From the sole of your foot, even unto the head there is no soundness in it, but wounds, and bruises, and putrefying sores. They have not been closed, neither bound up, neither mollified with ointment. And the daughter of Zion is left as a booth in a vineyard, as a lodge in a garden of cucumbers, as a besieged city. Except the LORD of Hosts had left unto us a very small remnant, we should have been like Sodom, and we should have been like Gomorrah." Does that sound like the *(tsadik ehbed)* the righteous servant of Isa. 53:11 or the servant extolled, exalted and elevated, one who could redeem, ransom and return Israel to the LORD?

Isaiah or *Yesha'yahu*'s theme is, "Israel's Messiah!" Therefore, he writes about the majestic glory of God. He foretells of the Messiah's; Birth 7:14; Deity 9:6-7; Ministry 42:1-7 & 61:1-2; Death 52:13-53:12; and Millennial Reign 2, 11, 65. He lived and ministered in Jerusalem with his wife a prophetess and his two sons *Shear-jashub* and *Maher-shalal-hash-baz*. We know nothing of his birth and death other than the Talmudic legend that wicked king Manasseh sawed him in half in a log at the pool of *Siloam*.

He was a writer, a poet, a statesman, a reformer, a teacher, a theologian, and a prophet referred to as, "The Shakespeare of Prophets. His theme is found in his name, "Salvation is of the LORD." The word salvation is found 26 times in Isaiah and only 7 times in all the other prophets combined. Isaiah is often referred to as, 'The Mini Bible.' The Bible has 66 books, Isaiah has 66 chapters, the Bible has 39 books in the Older Testament and 27 books in the Newer Testament.

Isaiah is divided into 39 chapters and 27 chapters and the middle chapter of the last 27 is chapter 53 and the central verse of that section in Isa. 53:5, "But He was wounded for our transgressions, He was bruised for our iniquities, the chastisement of our peace was upon Him, and with His stripes we are healed." (Coincidence or Providence?) Isaiah has been referred to as the, 'Fifth Gospel' or 'The Gospel According To Isaiah.' Isaiah 54:2-3 was the text William Carey, the father of modern missions used, to launch the modern missionary movement. Isaiah's first message of condemnation is aimed at his own people, the nation of Israel.

In chapter one we have a capsulized message of Isaiah, the breach between Israel and Jehovah; The inefficiency of mere ritual; The call to national repentance; and The certainty of sweeping judgment. Chapter 6 is Isaiah's call which is followed by chapters 7-12, 'The Book of Immanuel.' Then you have prophecies concerning Israel's neighbors in chapters 13-23; Prophecies about Israel's future in chapters 24-27; Prophecies of Israel's sinful 'WOES' in chapters 28-35; An historical parenthesis of King Hezekiah's life in chapters 36-39; Then you come to the prophecies concerning Israel's comfort in chapters 40-66 and these break down into three sections: The process of peace chapters 40-48; The Prince of peace chapters 49-57; and The program of peace chapters 58-66.

The "Crown Jewel" of the Older Testament in Isaiah 52:13-53:12 breaks down into five three verse couplets or triplets which is a Hebraic form of writing, worship and study: The Servant Exalted/Venerated Isa. 52:13-15; The Servant Despised/Villainized, Isa. 53:1-3; The Servant Wounded/Victimized, Isa. 53:4-6; The Servant Cut-Off/Vicarious, Isa. 53:7-9; The Servant Satisfied/Victorious, Isa. 53:10-12.

You also have: The Mystery of The Servant, Isa. 52:13-15; The Rejection of The Servant, Isa. 53:1-3; The Atonement of The Servant, Isa. 53:4-6; The Submission of The Servant, Isa. 53:7-9; and, The Exaltation of The Servant, Isa. 53:10-12. Then if you look real close you will also see the

'Five Levitical Offerings;' The Burnt Offering - The servant's whole hearted sacrifice, Isa. 52:13-15; The Meal Offering - The servant's perfect character, Isa. 53:1-3; The Peace Offering - The servant's atonement that brought peace with God, Isa. 53:4-6; The Sin Offering - The servant's payment for the transgression of his people, Isa. 53:7-9; The Trespass Offering - The servant's death for the effects of sin, Isa. 53:10-12.

However, no matter how you look at it or cut it up, the central element, the apex of this Messianic Prophecy is still, "The Servant!" The 'Suffering Servant' of the LORD, and He is the most important subject in the book of Isaiah as a whole. The Servant in this passage never speaks, nor does He ever appear. He is the object of discussion and haunts this passage.

After Isaiah chapter 53 the word servant, singular never appears again in Isaiah! In Exodus 3:5 as Moses approached the burning bush the Almighty spoke and said, "Draw not nigh, put off thy shoes from off thy feet, for the place whereon thou standest is holy ground." I believe we need that same attitude of reverence as we approach this 'Crown Jewel' and begin to examine its many facets. Like Philip in Acts 8:26-39 with the Ethiopian Eunuch when he, "Opened his mouth, and began at the same scripture (Isaiah 53:6-7) and preached unto him Jesus." Now let us lay this 'Crown Jewel' on a piece of black velvet under the jeweler's bright lights, pick up our monocle, take a deep prayerful breath and look deep into this gem's beauty for what *Jehovah Elohim* might have for each one of us.

Our main interest in Isaiah is the 'Crown Jewel' of the Older Testament, Isaiah 52:13-53:12. One that is purposely skipped every summer in the synagogues during their Torah and Haftorah readings. Our Jewish friends read Isaiah 51:12-52:12 and Deuteronomy 16:18-21:9. The next Sabbath they read Isaiah 54:1-10 and Deuteronomy 21:10-25:19, but they never read Isaiah 52:13-53:12, NEVER! Why?

Two reasons; **One,** because evangelical Christians use Isaiah 53 as the cornerstone for their argument for the *Messiahship of Yeshua*/Jesus. While Orthodox Jewish people on the other hand, follow the 11th C. Talmudic Rabbi, Rashi who said, "Since Christians interpret Isaiah 53 as being a prophecy concerning Jesus, we maintain that this is a prophecy concerning the people of Israel:" **Second**, because Isaiah chapter 53 is probably the most amazing, mystifying, powerful, passage of scripture in the Older Testament.

In fact it is so amazing and so mystifying and so powerful and so persuasive, that you need to be careful when approaching this passage that you don't accept the fact that *Yeshua/Jesus* is Israel's Messiah without accepting Him as your own personal Messiah too. Personal appropriation is critical, Joel 2:32, a head knowledge won't give anyone eternal life. Most of the 80 plus references in the Newer Testament referring to Isaiah, refer to Isaiah 53.

This is however, a matter of life and death, not just a matter for debate, or who has more evidence, or more convincing points. If Isaiah 53 is speaking of a suffering individual then the Jewish people failed to recognize their Messiah when *Yeshua/Jesus* of Nazareth came 2,000 years ago to save them. If however, it is speaking of a suffering Nation/Israel then Christians past, present and future who are laying claim to God's forgiveness through faith in the blood of Jesus are still in fact, "dead in their sins." Eph. 2:5. The answer to this question will not be found in sectarian name calling or in a lengthy theological debate but in a rational examination of the Biblical text and context of Isaiah chapter 53, the history of its interpretation and its relation to other prophecies whose messianic meaning is beyond dispute. However, you must remember this is only a study, not a theological journal or disputation. I am not here to argue, just share, as a common man to common men and women!

Chapter One: The Servant Exalted (Isa 52:13-15)

Part One: The Servant's Triumphal Entry – Isa. 52:13

Isaiah Fifty Three, "The Crown Jewel" of the Older Testament has captivated the hearts and minds of Bible students and scholars for centuries if not millenniums. Kyle Yates an O. T. Professor called it, "The Mt. Everest of Old Testament prophecy." Polycarp called it, "The golden passional of the Old Testament evangelist." Polycarp was a disciple of the apostle John, who was ordained by John, was the bishop of Smyrna, helped form the canon, and was martyred. C. H. Spurgeon said of this passage it's, "A Bible in miniature and the gospel in its essence." F. Delitzsch said, "It is the most central, deepest, loftiest thing Old Testament prophecy ever achieved, even out stripping itself...It looks as if it had been written beneath the cross on Golgotha." (Looking up at Christ, hanging on the nails).

"The Crown Jewel" which actually runs from, Isa. 52:13 – Isa. 53:12 is the fourth and final "Servant Song" of Isaiah: 42:1-7; 49:1-6; 50:4-9; 52:13- 53:12. It is divided into five stanzas of three verses each, with each stanza being longer than the previous one and the themes of exaltation and humiliation interwoven throughout each one beautifully. Exaltation dominates the first and last stanza and humiliation dominates the middle three, but the first verse of each stanza captures the theme of that stanza and seems to summarize its content.

You will notice references to the Levitical priesthood and the sacrificial system and because of that many believe the five stanzas are structured to match the five Levitical offerings: The Burnt Offering – Isa. 52:13-15; The Meal Offering – Isa. 53:1-3; The Peace Offering – Isa. 53:4-6; The Sin Offering – Isa. 53:7-9; and, The Trespass Offering – Isa. 53:10-12.

Before you can examine each facet of this "Crown Jewel" you must address a question that has been debated by theologians for centuries, both Jewish and Gentile, "Who is the suffering Servant?" So many suggestions have been put forth over the last thousand years that you could write a book on it, but only three are really worthy of any consideration and ultimately the context will be the assay test, or should I say 'acid text' for who the servant really is!

You see only Isaiah and Zechariah provide prophetic support for a 'Suffering Messiah.' **Corporately** – It is the nation or a remnant of Israel based on Isa. 49:3, "Thou art My servant, O Israel, in whom I will be glorified." This view was birthed by Rashi around 1100 AD between the two Crusades and developed in medieval Jewish thought but fails on two counts: 1 – The historical tradition of interpretation: 2 – The work accomplished by the Servant. Israel could not atone for their own sins, much less the sins of the world. **Individually** – It is Isaiah, Eliakim, David, Jeremiah, Zerubabbel or even Moses. However, the description of the Servant as you can see hardly fits the life and ministry of any of these Bible characters as great as they may have been, nor could Isa. 53:9b be said of any of them, "because he had done no violence, neither was any deceit in his mouth." **Messianically** – The suffering Servant is the coming Messiah, the Royal Davidic King, the ideal Israelite, who is totally committed and consecrated to Jehovah's will, work, plan and purpose for His life; and "..His soul became an (*asham*) a sin offering." Isa. 53:10b; "for the sins of the whole world." I John 2:2.

Gerhard von Rod, a professor at Heidelberg University in Germany said, "We may rule out those interpretations, some of which are grossly fanciful, that see in the Servant a figure in the past. The Servant embodies all that is good in Israel's existence before *Yahweh*, the expressions used go far beyond biography, and indeed they go far beyond the present. The picture of the Servant of *Yahweh*, of His mission to Israel and to the world, and of His expiatory suffering, is prophecy of the future and belongs to the realm of pure miracle which *Yahweh* reserved for Himself." I believe that Jesus in Mark 10:45 & Matt. 20:28, takes Isaiah 53, 'The Suffering Servant' and Dan. 7, 'The Son of Man' and performs a marriage ceremony right before our very eyes and weds together (Dan. 7:13-14 & Mark 14:62) and redefines for us who and what the Messiah would be. Dan. 9:24-27 and Isa. 52:13-53:12 are like a birthday invitation; Isa. 53 tells us who and what to look for and Dan. 9 tells us when and where the party is happening.

Isaiah 52:13, has 16 words in English but only 7 words in Hebrew; the first word in this 'Crown Jewel' is a particle of interjection, "Behold!" 'Look! Lo! See! Now! It is a marker used to enliven a narrative, to change a scene, to emphasize an idea or to call attention to detail. It's a word demanding attention to something or to point to something!

Imagine a group of soldiers standing outside of a building and talking and a general steps out and someone yells, **"ATTENTION!"** What do they do? Stand around with their hands in their pockets and keep talking, only if they want to go to the brig for insubordination. No, they snap to attention, face the general, look sharp and salute him! Now, that's the word we have here at the beginning of this crown jewel; "Behold, Look, Take notice; **ATTENTION**!!! My Servant..."

Anytime you come across this word in the Scriptures it would be wise to put a large **X** in the margin of your Bible with the letters R-R in it for rail/road crossing. When you come to a rail-road crossing sign there are three words on it, "Stop, Look, Listen!" For good reasons, a train might be coming and kill you! We need to heed that same warning in the Scriptures as we read God's word, when we come upon the words, 'Behold, Look, Lo, See, etc.

We need to, 'STOP' completely, 'Stop' immediately, (complete cessation of movement) and back up! 'LOOK' all around, 'Look' both ways, 'Look' up and down, look inside, look outside, look upside, look downside, look at the context, look up the words and get an idea of where you are in the Scriptures, (book, chapter, verse, pilcrow).

Then 'LISTEN' to that still, small voice of the Holy Spirit as He speaks to you from His Word and He still speaks if you will take time to be still and "LISTEN!" (Listening is a lost art today!) The words silent and listen have the exact same letters, but you have to be silent to listen.

The word 'Behold' is not there by coincidence or accident, it is there by **'Divine Design'** to call our attention to something of importance. "Behold My Servant..." I want you to Look at 'My Servant,' I want you to Focus on 'My Servant,' I want you to See 'My Servant,' I want you to Listen to 'My Servant!' **"BEHOLD, (*Hinneh*) My Servant!"**

Now who is the **"My?"** Well, it can't be Isaiah the author, because he doesn't have servants that we know of and the rule is, the closest antecedent in number, case and gender will identify it. So, we go back to verse 12 where we find the word LORD (*YHVH - Jehovah*). Now, remember in the original scrolls there were no chapter and verse divisions. The chapter divisions came in 1205 by Stephen Langton the Archbishop of Canterbury. The verse divisions came in 1551 by Robert Stephanus a printer. Classically the Bible scrolls have always been divided by blank spaces at the end or in the middle.

So, the pronoun 'My' must refer to Jehovah because He is the One who is speaking in chapter 52:3, 4 & 5. He is also mentioned by name in 52:9, 10, 11 & 12 and I don't think we have any argument from either side of the river on that point anyway so we can keep on fishing and that leads us to the third word in the first phrase of the first verse, "**Servant**." Since the servant is not identified as Isaiah or Israel, etc. we will have to allow the context to identify just who it is, and we can reduce it to three, Israel, an individual or the Messiah.

We can't go back three chapters to Isa. 49:3 and pull out a verse we like and make an application, that would be poor exegesis, in fact that's also poor eisegesis, no matter what your bias is! So, we will have to let scripture interpret scripture and let the word of God speak for itself, Amen? (That was weak!) I don't believe God's word needs defense attorneys and that is the purpose of studying to take this passage apart word by word and let it speak to the common man from the common man. What's interesting in this passage, which we will note, is that sometimes 'The Servant' is spoken of; Sometimes He's spoken to; However, He never speaks for Himself; If He would it would solve the problem and we will try to point those out as we go along.

"**...shall deal prudently (*sa-kal*)...**" or He shall, behave wisely; guide wittingly; to have insight, wisdom and understanding; to be extremely wise in all decisions. He who deals wisely will obtain success. This servant would grow from childhood and become strong in spirit, filled with wisdom, and the grace of God. (Luke 2:40; 52)

Knowledge is the mere acquisition of facts, you get knowledge from college. Wisdom is taking knowledge and applying it to life and making it work, putting feet on your diploma. Wisdom is what enables us to use knowledge correctly. Knowledge is knowing a tomato is a fruit, wisdom is knowing not to use it in a smoothie. Without knowledge, college is a waste of time and money. This servant would not only behave wisely; but the Hebrew word (*sa-kal*) means he would also teach others knowledge also.

It is one thing to teach academics but you have to be extremely wise to teach knowledge because you only learn knowledge from life, and from experience, not from books. You learn facts from books, you learn how to act and live from God's book. Einstein said, "Wisdom is not the product of schooling, but the lifelong attempt to acquire it." Tennyson said, "Knowledge comes but wisdom lingers." Truth stays with a person for the rest of their life coloring all their thoughts and actions. School teaches us how to make a living, the Bible teaches us how to live.

My best teachers were those who spent 25 years in the jungles, on the streets and in the pulpits first and then taught from their own experience! The verb (*sa-kal*) includes both intelligent and effective action; success does not result from lack of effort, but from effective action. This servant is experienced, seasoned, knowledgeable, accomplished, and skillful and He is an expert in every field. He will be so wise, so prudent; he will be teaching knowledge, not facts. His mission will be successful; in fact this thought is introduced before the servant and not mentioned again until the tenth verse of the next chapter.

This word (*sa-kal*) portrays a word picture of a man crossing his arms and hands in an extended motion showing total contentment with his instruction, wisdom and insight to his disciples. **Knowledge is the tool you get from school; wisdom is the crafts, the skill, the art you get from life.**

"He shall be exalted and extolled, and be very high." He shall be Exalted (*rum*) noble, raised up, lifted up;" Then he is going to go higher; "he will be 'extolled' (*nasa*) lifted up higher and honored; extolled is a reflexive verb to lift or raise oneself up." (John 12:32).   E. J. Young says, 'It's referring to the ascension, to raise Himself.' Yet this servant is still going to go higher, "He will be exalted, extolled and be 'very high' (*me-od ga-bah*) exceedingly, utterly high or elevated to honor. "And I, if I be lifted up from the earth, will draw all men unto me." John 12:32. I can't help but wonder if 'NASA' (National Aeronautics Space Administration) took their acrostic from this Hebrew word.

These three verbs are used to convey the absolute height this servant shall attain, the highest of the highest! Above the angels, principalities, & powers. When you put all three of these verbs together this is what you get. He will rise up; He will raise Himself still higher; He will stand as the highest possible being ever! So, you have the commencement, the continuation and the climax of his exaltation. Not only that, but this last word 'very high' is a perfect tense showing at last he has reached an immeasurable height, the pinnacle, the apex, the joy that was set before him, Heb. 12:2, "the right hand of the throne of God."

What's interesting is the Scriptures talk about the first, second and third heaven. The one where God dwells and the words 'Exalted and Extolled' high and lifted up are used in combination four times in Isaiah and no where else in the Older Testament to refer to it. Also the other three references all refer to God!

Isaiah writes in Isa. 33:10, "Now will I **rise**, (*qum*) saith the LORD, now will I be **exalted**, (*ramam*) now will I **lift up** (*nasa*) myself." God is speaking of Himself, not Isaiah or David or Israel and He uses the same exact three words found in Isa. 52:13 used of the servant, but here they are used for *(Jehovah)* Himself. "The LORD – Jehovah – **YHWH**." In Isa. 6:1 you have similar language again, Isaiah is speaking of the Lord (*Adonai*) "I saw also the Lord sitting upon a throne, **high** (*rum*) and **lifted up** (*nasa*) and his train filled the temple." The exact same words used in Isa. 52:13 for the Servant but here they are used for Lord *(Adonai)*. Isaiah writes in 57:15, "For thus says the **high** (*rum*) and **lofty** (*nasa*) One who inhabits eternity, whose name is Holy; I dwell in the **high** (*marom*) and holy place, with him also who is of a contrite and humble spirit, to revive the spirit of the humble, and to revive the heart of the contrite ones." "The Lofty One, The Holy One, The One True God, ***Elohim***." v.21. Isaiah writes in Isa. 52:13, "Behold, my servant shall deal prudently; he shall be **exalted** (*rum*) and **extolled**, (*nasa*) and be **very high** (*me-od ga-bah*)." "My Servant, ***Maschiach***." These words are not found anywhere else in the prophets in this combination, except here.

Whoever this servant is in Isa. 52:13-53:12 He is on equal footing with *Adonai* in Isa. 6:1; *Jehovah* in Isa. 33:10; *Elohim* in Isa. 57:15 and He is going to be exalted, extolled and elevated. Higher than any being, creature or creation that has ever been exalted in all the universe. It will be absolute and beyond comprehension and the writer uses three verbs to show the progress of this ascending exaltation higher and higher, to the highest of the highest (*marom*) the highest in honor, status and exaltation, being in an elevated position on highest of the highest!

Isaiah combines these verbs to show elevation of exaltation; the idea is that this Servant would be elevated to the highest pitch of honor. (A word used to express a musical note). The word 'exalted' is often synonymous with praise but here it is used to elevate him to the highest conceivable position imaginable, 'The right hand of God Almighty on high!' Can you fathom that? Can you? This is beyond my finite mind to comprehend! ***"Behold, My Servant, shall deal prudently; He shall be exalted and extolled, and be very high."*** Maybe that's why it took ten days from the ascension Acts 1:11 to the outpouring of the Holy Spirit Acts 2:33 to be completed.

****

Part Two: The Servant's Terrifying Exit – Isa. 52:14

Isaiah 52:13 deals with the Servant's, 'Triumphal Entry,' he was exalted, extolled and elevated. Lifted high, higher and finally highest above any being ever in all of existence. The Jewish Sages in Yalkut ii: 571, in the 13th c. wrote concerning this Servant, "Who art thou, O great mountain?" A reference to, Zech. 4:7; It was referring to King Messiah, and why does he call Him, "The Great Mountain?" Because He is greater than the patriarchs, as it is said, "My servant shall be high, and lifted up, and lofty exceedingly" - He will be higher than Abraham...lifted up above Moses...loftier than the ministering angels." Says, Driver & Neubauer. Isaiah 52:14 will deal with His 'Terrifying Exit' and v.15 will deal with His 'Tremendous Eulogy.' So, we have his 'Triumphal Entry' in v.13; His 'Terrifying Exit' in v.14; And his 'Tremendous Eulogy' in v.15.

What is interesting is, the word servant is used 22 times in Isaiah and the word servants is used 17 times. What's unique is when the LORD refers to an individual as His servant, He gives us their name; Isaiah 20:3; Eliakim 22:20; David 37:35, etc. When He refers to Israel being the servant, He clarifies it by adding the name Jacob or Israel, 41:8, 41:9, 42:19 & 24; 43:1 & 10; 44:1 & 2; 44:21 & 26; 48:20; 49:3 & 5; nine out of ten times! Only once does He fail to do that!

However, when the LORD refers to His individual Servant, the Messiah or Redeemer, He doesn't add a name or a nation as in Isaiah. 42:1; 49:5, 6 & 7; 50:10; 52:13; 53:11. In fact in Isaiah 42:1-7 we see a two-fold account of His Servant as weak, despised, rejected and slain but also as a mighty conqueror taking vengeance on the Gentile nations and restoring Israel.

In Matt. 12:14-21 in the Newer Testament, Isa. 42:1-7 is quoted and *Yeshua/Jesus* applies it to Himself as He is healing all the people and charges them 'NOT' to make Him known! This total divergence in Messianic prophecies has led ancient Rabbis to promote a two Messiah theory: A suffering Messiah Isa. 50:5-7 & 53, 'Messiah ben Joseph' who dies in battle; and a triumphant Messiah, Psalm 2 & 110, 'Messiah ben David' who will establish the 'Kingdom of Righteousness' after defeating the Gentile nations.

While Christians see it as the Messiah's two comings or two advents; The first as a 'Suffering Servant' and the second as the 'Sovereign King.' The first time He will come as a lowly servant, riding on a baby donkey, Zech. 9:9 to be executed; The second time He will come as the 'King of kings' riding on a white horse, Rev. 19:11-16 to execute judgment. Polycarp referred to Isaiah 53 as, "The Golden Passional, or the Holy of Holies of the Older Testament." Many who have studied it say, it is like sitting under the cross on Calvary with Christ hanging on the nails and looking up at Him and writing exactly what you see.

"As many were astounded (*shaw-mem*) at thee..." (This is still spoken by the voice of Deity! Jehovah is still talking!) This first line portrays public reaction to the servant and the second line gives us the reaction for that reaction. "They were horrified at what they saw!" Isa. 52:14 says many were, astonished, appalled, awestruck, horrified; this word means to stun, to grow numb, to be devastated, to stupefy; to tremble from fear or horror, to be terrified!

The primary idea here is, they were struck dumb with sudden astonishment and there begins a contrast in this verse that is completed in the next one and in the last two verses in the next chapter; Isa. 53:11 & 12, where the Servant will, "justify the many" and "bare the sin of the many." Or as one author put it, "This word expresses deep, bewildered amazement caused by the transformation of the marred, distorted, beyond human resemblance of the servant's visage!" This isn't a few people that are in shock, frozen from fear or horror, by an incredible, unbelievable, devastation; the word many (*ra-bah*) means abundant, numerous, great, multitudes; The world, like the 'Holocaust!'

This same word is used in Ezek. 26:16 and 27:35 to describe men's reaction to the ruins of Tyre after Nebuchadnezzer destroyed it, tore it to the ground and left the rubble to be thrown into the sea 300 years later by Alexander to build a causeway out to the island to destroy the remnant. His appearance was such as to excite universal astonishment and produce universal disgust. Or as one translator put it, "Many individuals were petrified by paralyzing astonishment, "At Thee!" The Servant, but why? Why were they petrified? Why were they paralyzed? What was shocking was, this was the One they cried, "Hosanna, Blessed is the King of Israel, that comes in the name of the Lord," John 12:12, on Monday and there He is hanging on a cross between two gangsters on Friday with a sign over his head in Hebrew, Greek and Latin which read, "Jesus Of Nazareth, The King Of The Jews!" John 19:19. It seems strange that the Jewish people ignore the fact that these words were written in Hebrew first and reading from right to left they would read, ***"Yeshua Hanozri Wumelech Hajehudim"*** Religious scholars even today emphasize the first letter in each Hebrew word and try to find their hidden meaning. What they saw was "Y,H,W,H" the holy name for their eternal God, the Creator of heaven and earth, Jehovah! It was a shock and they protested, "Write not, 'The king of The Jews, but he said I am the king of the Jews" Jn. 19:21. Pilate responded, "What I have written, I have written." John 19:22.

"His visage was so marred, more than any man... " The Hebrew word for man is (*ish* – nobility, great men, men of high degree, we'll see it again in v.3). In Isaiah 52:13 we have the good news about the servant, "He was Exalted, Extolled and Elevated..." But in v.14 we have the bad news, the ugly news, the news that will, stun you, devastate you and leave you numb and speechless. In v.14 we have suffering that borders on the unthinkable!

"His visage (*mar-eh*) was so marred..." His appearance, his shape, his looks, his comeliness, his face, "was **sooo** marred..." Not just marred or distorted, but **sooo** marred! This word marred (*mishat or moshat*) means deformity, defect, corruption, disfigurement, implying ugliness and repulsion. More than any man ever in the history of the world! Why, because any other man would have died early on, in this horrible, tortuous beating, but He couldn't, because He never sinned and death is the result of sin. Rom. 5:12.

He did not even look human, this was the effect of the brutalities mentioned in Matt. 26:67; 27:27-30; Mk. 14:65 where he was 'buffeted' to rap with the fist over and over and over! In Luke 22:63-66; and John 19:1 you have the scourging with the 'cat of nine tails;' 39 stripes, or 40 save one was only for Roman citizens which *Yeshua Jesus* was not! Isa. 50:6, "I gave my back to the smiters, and my cheeks to them that plucked off the hair; I hid not my face from shame and spitting"

Or as one author put it, "His disfigurement was so grotesque, His appearance was hardly human!" Thus people were paralyzed with wonder at the horror of His suffering and at the extent of the cruelty inflicted upon this Servant by them. Oh the awesome cost of our redemption! Can you even begin to fathom it, to comprehend its cost?

Matthew Henry so aptly stated: "His visage was marred more than any man's when He was buffeted, smitten on the cheek and crowned with thorns and hid not His face from shame and spitting. His face was foul with weeping, for He was a man of sorrows; He that really was fairer than the children of men had His face spoiled with the abuses that were done to Him."

Never was a man abused so barbarously, as this Servant and never did a man look so miserable, "a worm and no man." Ps. 22:6; "His own nation abhorred Him," Isa. 49:7; and treated Him as the off-scouring of all things. Never was there sorrow like His sorrow, "a man of sorrows, acquainted with grief," Isa. 53:3.

There are no words to describe this, "despised, rejected, man of sorrows, acquainted with grief." None! The Hebrew word for acquainted is (*yada* – intimate, personal acquaintance) Messiah/Servant meet grief, pain, sorrow, spitting, insults, sin; grief, sorrow, pain, spitting, sin meet Messiah/Servant, get intimate with each other!

It is interesting to note that before Constantine made Christianity the state religion, all forms of art of Jesus Christ were plain, worn, lean and without earthly beauty. There was nothing in the 'Son of Man' to attract mankind because God wanted mankind to come of his own free will to the Savior. He was not a charismatic individual, just plain vanilla, no sprinkles, a robe and sandals!

"...and his form more than the sons of men--" The Hebrew word for men is (*adom* – ruddy, mankind, ordinary men, human being) this is not the word for noble men. The word marred is used of a blemished animal unfit for sacrifice, disfigured, ruined, battered or decaying. The reason for the brutal beating was to make him unfit for sacrifice or to kill him before his time, before 3:00 pm the time of the evening offering, or the 'Passover Lamb' sacrifice!

Even His beard was ripped out by the roots, Isaiah 50:6-7. (The 3rd Servant Song) Not only was his visage, his face so distorted but his form, (*to-ar*) his outline, his figure, his shape, his frame or likeness was distorted beyond or "more than the sons of men..." So as not to belong to men or not to be one of the human family, then what was it?

Keil & Delitzsch stated, "His appearance and his form were altogether distorted away from man, out beyond men." (Beyond a human being) E.J. Young said, "His disfigurement was so great that he no longer appeared as a man." That is a distortion that destroyed all likeness to a man, think about that for a moment! He didn't even look human! We get a glimpse into the depth of the intense suffering of this Servant, which transfigured His whole image beyond human resemblance – He didn't even look human anymore! A grotesque form hung on the cross! Think of the sin offering on the altar; what do you see? An ugly, bloody slab of meat!

So if, **'IF'** *Yeshua/Jesus* was that Servant and if He went through that horrible execution and did not look human, what was up there on that cross? Some flesh and blood and bones; A slab of meat, and the slab talked, seven or eight times and one of those times it said, "Father, forgive them, for they know not what they do!" (Ten words that changed the philosophy of the world!)

How could an innocent <u>human being</u> utter those ten words that changed the philosophy of the world for all time? Unthinkable, unimaginable, inconceivable! It was not just the physical punishment that deformed His image, NO! It was also the emotional, mental, spiritual trauma internally that deformed this pure, sinless, 'Holy God' that was to become 'Sin' for you and for me! That's what really distorted His face and frame, our SIN! I believe that did more damage to Him than the whip, the nails, the thorns, or the spear!

What did He mean in Matt. 26:38 when He said to His disciples, "My soul (*psyche*) is exceedingly sorrowful, even unto death; tarry here and watch with Me." He is going to sweat great drops of blood, (*hematohidrosis*) Dr. Luke 22:44; He will pray with strong tears and crying, before dying, Heb. 5:7 (*ischyros* – strong, powerful, mighty, forceful tears); An angel was sent to strengthen Him, Luke 22:43. You can see the answer in, Isa. 53:10, 11 & 12; when His soul (*nephesh/nefesh*) is made a trespass offering, and Jehovah sees the birth pangs of His soul and is satisfied and He pours out His soul unto death, bare naked.

Don't lose the shock value as you study this "Crown Jewel" that this disfigured King of creation is your Lord and Savior; It had to be! John 20:27-28, He has the scars to prove it, the only man-made thing in heaven! Listen, if you aspire to be a servant of His, you will pick up some scars along the way too, scars are part of the deal! Gal. 6:17, Paul said, "I bear in my body the marks of the Lord Jesus."

Now how anyone, anyone; Jew, Gentile, Christian, Agnostic, Atheist, Muslim, Buddhist, Hindu, New Age, anyone can read the torture inflicted upon this 'holy, harmless, undefiled, servant of God' without pathos, without being moved to tears, without feeling something, is beyond me. My Jewish grandmother's entire family was butchered in a Pogrom in southern Poland and hunted down and some-how she managed to escape at 11 years old and was smuggled to America by two Roman Catholic Nuns and as horrible as that was, it doesn't even begin to compare to this image. Six million innocent Jewish men, women and children were burned up in the ovens of the holocaust and as repulsive and repugnant as that is it does not compare to this. A holy, pure, innocent God made into sin for us!

Maybe, just maybe that's why he cried from the tree, "Woman, behold thy son!" Because, as she looked up there she said, "That's not my son, in fact that's not even a human being up there!" The world was in shock with what they witnessed, horrified, dumbstruck, frozen in terror. Why? Because a man was beaten and nailed to a tree! Because an innocent man was stripped naked and executed without a fair trial! That stuff happens every day in this godless world!

No, because this Servant took the cup of Almighty God's wrath and judgment and lifted it up with both hands and thanked Him for it and with one mighty gulp, drank damnation dry for every man, woman and child that would ever be born. Then He climbed up on our tree and with all the strength He had left He stretched one hand up to God and the other out to man and said, "Father, forgive them, for they know not what they do!"

This Servant didn't go to the tree because it was fun, No my friend! He went because it had to be done! There just was no other way to pay the debt for mankind's sin! NONE!! Don't you think if there was some other way possible for God to take care of our redemption He would have done it? Don't you? I Do!

"For He God, made Him Christ, Who knew no sin, to be sin for us, that we might be made, the righteousness of God in Him." II Cor. 5:21 (He took your Hell so you could have His Heaven!) The Gospel message is not that 'Christ Died' that's history, Caesar died, Napolean died, Lincoln died. The Gospel message is, "Christ died for our sins according to the scriptures;" I Cor. 15:1-5. You and I are as guilty of this Servants death as, Annas, Caiaphas, Herod, Pilate and the Soldiers who beat Him and nailed Him to the cross and the ones who spit in His face; because it was our sin, yours and mine that put Him there!

Part Three: The Servant's Tremendous Eulogy – Isa. 52:15

In v. 13 we see the Servant's, 'Triumphal Entry;' He was exalted, extolled and elevated far above what any being could ever imagine. In v. 14 we see the Servant's, 'Terrifying Exit;' He was so marred, so deformed, so distorted, so mutilated, "more than any man" ever in history. In v. 15 we see the Servant's, 'Tremendous Eulogy;' His life and message will cover the earth 'from the lowest of men to the highest of kings.' <u>The astonishment of His disfigurement is turned into the amazement of His grace and glory</u>!

In v.14 'many' individuals were Astonished; But in v.15 'many' nations would be 'Aspersed or Sprinkled.' Here Isaiah compares the previous distorted, marred appearance of the Servant, with the high priestly position of the One who would cleanse mankind from sin's defilement. Many see His disfigurement as punishment for His own sin but it was a condition that would bring cleansing to the nations, it was a punishment for all mankind's sin.

<u>The suffering now becomes the pathway to glory</u>! I don't know how it all works, I don't, but God is glorified when we suffer, glorified! Acts 5:41; 9:16; Rom. 8:18; 2 Cor. 4:17; Jam. 5:10; I Pet. 2:20; 5:10. (Listen, if God has called you to suffer, then suffer and be quiet!) Paul said in Phil. 3:10, "That I may know (*ginosko* – experiential knowledge) Him, and the power of His resurrection, and the fellowship of His suffering, being made conformable unto His death." God said of Paul in Acts 9:16, "For I will show him how great things he must suffer for My names sake." The disciples rejoiced because they were counted worthy to suffer shame for his name. Acts 5:41. Read Rom. 8:18 or Paul's testimony in 2 Cor. 11:23-27, then think about how really bad you have it!

"**So shall he sprinkle many (*rabah*) nations (*goi'im*);**" In the Bible there are only two kinds of people Jews and Gentiles/*Goi'im*, and the Gentiles/*Goi'im* are going to get sprinkled. The word sprinkle is the Hebrew word (*nazah*) and is a technical term in the Mosaic law for the sprinkling of blood, for ceremonial cleansing of sin. (It is an imperfect verb, *yaz-zeh* from *nazah*) **Contextually** there is support for the translation of (*nazah*) as sprinkled; As priestly and sacrificial themes run throughout this passage.

Rhetorically there seems to be a comparison between v. 14 where the many are shocked at the Servants abuse; and v. 15 where they are shocked at the Servants accomplishments, which lends support to the translation of 'startle' for some translators.

This has prompted some to translate (*nazah*) in Isa. 52:15 as, 'startle' a possible translation but the context and all other texts demand 'sprinkle' not 'startle.' Lev. 4:6. However, sprinkling with blood, oil or water was done for cleansing and consecration. Ex.29:21; Lev. 4:6; 8:11; 14:7. The verb 'sprinkle' means, "too scatter a liquid in small drops," and its usage is confined to a ceremonial act, Lev. 4:6. As the <u>Servant King</u> was shunned by 'the many' as unclean, so the <u>Servant Priest</u> shall sprinkle 'the many' (metaphorically) to make them clean. In Numbers 19, the clean shall sprinkle the unclean, making the unclean clean, and the clean unclean until evening, funny how that works.

This is a picture of this Servant taking our punishment so we could take His reward, "For He (God) has made Him (Christ) who knew no sin, to be sin for us, that we might be made the righteousness of God in Him (Christ)." II Cor. 5:21. In other words He took your hell so you could have His heaven. Wilson's Old Testament Dictionary says, "The uniform use of this word is in the sense of sprinkling with blood in order to purify." Young says, "The meaning of sprinkle here is atonement, *via* the sprinkling of blood." Victor Buksbazen says, "This word is used to describe the ritual of a leper by means of sprinkling the blood of a sacrifice, Lev. 14:7; or by the priest before the veil, Lev. 4:6." The Talmud refers to the Servant in Isa. 53:4 & 8 as 'The leprous one' (*nagua*) which will be discussed in detail later. He shall purify whole nations by His blood and present them holy to God, which is a legal sprinkling by which people are sanctified, or set apart to God.

Though shunned like a leper He now brings cleansing to the nations through His own blood atonement, not that of animals, but his own blood! (Powerful Thought!) This establishes the most important application of this passage to the virtue of the Messiah's, or the Servant's atonement.

Some Jewish interpreters translate (*nazah*) as startle, to cause to leap like a cat, to jump back suddenly which is probably an Arabic translation, not a Hebrew one. However, in all of the 24 passages where the Hebrew word (*nazah/yaz-zeh*) appears in the Bible it is translated sprinkle 17 times, and sprinkled 7 times. It is never translated in the Scriptures startled, once! So using the, "Law of First Mention" and the "Science of Etymology" they have a problem, but I can understand their choice. Sixteen times it refers to sprinkling blood, three times to sprinkling oil, two times to sprinkling water, two times to sprinkling water with the ashes of the Red Heifer and only one time in all of the Scriptures does it **not** specifically tell us what is being sprinkled. 'Only One Time!' So the context must determine what is being sprinkled; and that one time is right here, in our text, in Isa. 52:15, "So shall He sprinkle many nations."

The word (*nazah*) means to sprinkle in expiation, or in the act of atonement, and this has been proven throughout the Scriptures. To say the nations will be startled like a cat and jump back in shock doesn't fit the context! There were two kinds of sprinkling under the Mosaic law, the sprinkling of blood on and toward the mercy-seat, God-ward; and the sprinkling of water or oil on or toward the Levite or leper, man-ward. *So, the work of this Servant has this double aspect also.*

Gesenius believes the word sprinkle (*nazah*) universally in the Older Testament means either to sprinkle blood as the high priest makes expiation in, Lev. 4:6; or with water for purification in, Ezk. 36:25; Both of which are appropriate to the Messiah, John 13:8; Heb. 9:13-14; 10:22; 12:24; I Pet. 1:2. He will sprinkle 'many nations' not just Israel but (*rabah*) a great, many, number of nations (*Goyim*) Gentiles, peoples or generations, Gen. 10:1. Not just many, but every nation. Muilenberg states, "It is best to retain 'sprinkle' here as this interpretation is supported by the Manuel of Discipline, in the recently discovered 'Dead Sea Scriptures." Way before the 'MT' Masoretic Text. Also sprinkle carries the idea of purification, hence Lamsa's translation of the *Peshitta*, "he will purify many people from their sins." Knox also translates this, "He will purify a multitude of nations." (Some say this is not possible)

Well we can see a literal fulfillment of this prediction in I Peter 1:1-2 where people of many nations are described as having been sprinkled with the blood of Jesus Christ: "Peter an apostle of Jesus Christ, to the strangers (sojourners) scattered throughout Pontus, Galatia, Cappadocia, Asia, and Bithynia; Elect according to the foreknowledge of God, the Father, through the sanctification of the Spirit, unto obedience and **sprinkling of the blood**

of Jesus Christ: Grace unto you, and peace, be multiplied." Now was this a literal sprinkling or was it meant to be used metaphorically or spiritually by Peter? The Jewish Targum has, "So shall he scatter many nations..." representing sprits of water. It may be that this word (*nazah*) had a broader Hebrew meaning in ancient times than it does today and sprinkle, startle, scatter, or marvel as in the Septuagint were acceptable. However, the context must be what determines our interpretation when the plain sense does not make common sense and the context is one of 'sacrifice' not 'surprise.'

"...the kings (*melek*) shall shut (*kaw-fats*) their mouths (*peh*) at him;" The kings (*melek*) royal rulers, human or divine, the more prominent leader in a covenant agreement. In v.14 you have 'the many,' the people, the populace, but here you have the royalty, the rulers, the elite. You see this again in Isa. 53:3 with the word (*yish*) men of nobility, rulers, leaders, who despised and rejected this Servant. Here we have Kings who, "shall shut, stop, close their mouths at Him;" They shall cover their mouths, 'from the lowest of men to the highest of kings,' men were dumb founded with reverential awe and veneration with what they saw and heard of this Servant.

The idea here is that He would be honored, revered and respected by kings and noblemen. But not by all, and not at first, another evidence that *Yeshua* was the Messiah, "He was despised and rejected of men (*yish*)..." men of nobility, rank, honor, status, but not by all. Pilate tried to release Him four times and Joseph of Arimathaea and Nicodemus came for His body in John 19:38-42. Even Pilate tried to release Him four times but to no avail!

To shut their mouths here indicates veneration and admiration. Like, Job 29:9-10, "The princes refrained from talking, and laid their hands on their mouth. The nobles held their peace, and their tongue cleaved to the roof of their mouth." (They were speechless!) Kings shall be silent and dumb before Him out of profound humility, reverence and admiration for His wisdom and regal royalty.

"For that which had 'not' been told (*saw-far*) them shall they see (*ra`ah*)..." The word 'told' (*saw-far*) proclaimed, declared, inscribed, means to score with a mark using a penknife; it's the word for a scribe or writer. So, it means to leave an indelible mark on your heart, mind and soul, permanently! The Gospel does that, it changes people's lives, forever! "No change, No Jesus!" "No Jesus, No Change! Once you have heard the "Gospel" you can never be the same again, never! The Chinese word for Gospel is made up of two words, "Happiness from on High."

The word see (*ra'ah*) means to gaze upon, to consider, to stare at, to approve, to behold or realize, to take in and advise oneself. (*To see with the eyes of faith!*) All this in v.14 the Servant/Messiah has done for you, the spear, the spit, the thorns, the whip, the nails, the buffeting, the mockery, the nakedness, the flies, the loneliness, the suffocation, the pain, the thirst, the alienation, the sin, the darkness, etc., etc. **What** have you ever done for Him? **What?** If you were to stand before Him today, **What** would you lay at His feet? **What?**

So that which has been declared, will finally be realized and absorbed. They were never told; the only true God was the Jewish God, Elohim! Gentiles worshipped gods of gold, silver, wood, stone, brass, bronze and paper much like today! There's only one true God today, the Jewish God, that's why the world hates Israel. Christians worship His Son, *Yeshua/Jesus*, Israel's Messiah, the Servant in our study. Nothing has changed in this world, as Solomon said in Ecc. 1:9, "There is no new thing under the sun."

Albert Barnes explains that in this part of the verse a reason is given for the veneration of the kings. Here they receive intelligence of this wonderful Servant of God which had not been made known to them as it had been to the Jewish people, 'they shall see (*ra`ah*) what wasn't told them,' before.

"...and that which they had not heard (*sh'ma*) shall they consider (*bine*)." To hear intelligently, with understanding. It's not that they never heard about it, but it was never presented to them in a way they could understand. This word has the implication that they are paying attention now because of what happened in v.14 and they are now willing to trust and obey the message. Deut. 6:4, is called the ***"Sh`ma"*** for the Jewish people, "Hear, O Israel: The LORD our God is one LORD."

They had never heard of salvation of the Gentiles before which was not only new to them but strange and incredible to the Jewish people as well. Not only that but this "mystery...was kept secret since the world began," Rom. 16:25. The other mystery kept hidden in God from the beginning of the ages was the church, Jew and Gentile believers as one body Eph. 3:1-12; 2:14-18; Gal. 3:26-28; Col. 3:10-11.

"Shall they consider (*bine*)" which means to separate mentally, to distinguish, discern, ponder, and understand fully. The phrase, "they shall consider (*bine*)," is added here to show that 'seeing' in the former clause was meant of discerning those things with the eyes of their minds. In other words, the incarnation and redemption would contain truths and wonders they had not contemplated elsewhere.

No such events would have occurred within the range of their observation, and the wonders of redemption would stand by themselves as unparalleled in all that they had heard or seen. These kings and noblemen had never heard nor considered, 'That through the loss of all things including His own life, this Servant would conquer all things, including death.'

What is here predicted has been fulfilled; The mystery of the incarnation and the atonement; The sufferings and the death of the Redeemer; His exaltation and His glory, are events which are unparalleled in the history of the world. These are events fitted in their very nature to excite the profoundest admiration and to induce kings and nobles to lay their hands on their mouths in a token of veneration, and consider something they never heard nor saw before.

Or as one writer put it, "That which they had not paid much attention to, shall they diligently and cunningly view and know in their hearts and minds." Our hearts, minds and spirits must be enlightened to know the reason for Christ's sufferings and death. Just knowing that He died and suffered is nothing more than historical knowledge. We need to know why He suffered, why He died, why He came in the flesh? What was the need of the atonement, and what virtue was there in His sacrifice? Not to teach others but for our soul! Atonement is the propitiation, the satisfying sacrifice, whereby God through the death, burial and resurrection of His

Servant, Jesus Christ makes unholy men holy. (That is the 'Good News' of the Gospel!)

"He shall sprinkle many," but not all. There is no universal salvation here, the tree on Calvary settled that once and for all! "Many were astonished," but not all. "Many will be judged eternally," but not all! Those that have truly believed in the Servant of the LORD, and have truly repented of their sins, and have truly received Him into their hearts and lives: Those that have been and still are terrified at the vicious, torturous death of the Servant: Those that have been sprinkled with the blood of the Servant in v.14: Those are the ones who will receive Eternal Life, "and ... dwell in the house of the LORD forever!" Psalm 23:6, **But not all**!

Those are the ones who will experience fullness of joy and pleasure forever more. Psalm 16:11: But not all. Up to this point all the Messianic prophecies concerning salvation have been veiled! But now they are both perceived, understood and unveiled! This Servant, Israel's Messiah is going to 'Die a Terrible, Horrible Death!' To make atonement for the nations, the Goi'im, the Gentiles as well as Israel, 'the apple of His eye.' This is the first time in all of the Scriptures that this is clearly revealed. "For since the beginning of the world, men have not heard, nor perceived by the ear, neither has the eye seen, O God, beside thee, what He has prepared for him who waits for him." Isa. 64:4

PRAYER - "*Abba*, Father, how can we even begin to comprehend what Your Spirit has inspired Your prophet to write in these verses, when brilliant men have struggled with them for centuries? We are just common, humble men who come to You, Father and ask You to open our hearts and minds to Your infinite truths as we dip our tin cup into Your fathomless well for a sip of Your living water. Teach us Holy Spirit what it is You wish us to learn from this passage today that we might take something with us, something that would change our lives forever. *In ha shem Yeshua we pray. Amen!*"

Chapter Two: The Servant Despised (Isa 53:1-3)

Part One: The Servant's Arm Revealed – Isa. 53:1

Isaiah 53:1 flows naturally out of Isaiah 52:15. The speaker seems to be the redeemed community, led by redeemed Israel through the voice of her prophet. They look back and lament and mourn over the fact that they misjudged the Lord's Servant and did not believe the message about Him. The nations did not believe because they did not know! Israel knew and yet she did not believe because she failed to recognize the, "arm of the Lord" when it was revealed in the, "Suffering Servant." Both John, in John 12:38 and Paul in Rom. 10:16 saw in the unbelief of Israel a fulfillment of Isaiah 53:1. The English translations which use the 'past tense' throughout these verses accurately reflect the 700 years before Christ. The work of the Servant was a signed, sealed, and settled reality. Men may misunderstand Him, but God is made known through Him!

What is it that *Yeshua/Jesus* revealed to the two disciples on the road to Emmaus in Luke 24:25-27? "Then He said unto them, "O foolish ones, and slow of heart to believe all that the prophets have spoken! Ought not Christ to have suffered these things and to enter into His glory?" And beginning at Moses and all the prophets, He expounded unto them, in all the scriptures, the things concerning Himself." (What things?)

For centuries "Isaiah Fifty Three" has been excluded from the weekly reading cycles of Scripture in the Jewish Synagogues. In *Av/August* they end reading Isaiah 52:12 and begin the next Sabbath reading Isaiah 54:1. Why? Because 'Evangelical Christians' contend that <u>Isaiah 53</u> reveals the Messiahship of *Yeshua/Jesus* and Jewish people follow the 11th century Talmudic commentator, Rashi. Who said, "Since Christians interpret Isa. 53 as being a prophecy concerning Jesus, we maintain that it's a prophecy concerning the people of Israel." So, that solves the problem, or does it?

There is much more at stake here than debating different points of view. In fact, this is a matter of eternal spiritual life or eternal spiritual death! If this passage is speaking of a suffering individual, the Servant of God, then the Jewish people are wrong and have failed to recognize their Messiah almost 2,000 years ago and are dead in their trespasses and sins.

However, if it is speaking of the suffering nation of Israel, then Christians who have laid claim to God's forgiveness through faith in *Yeshua*/Jesus as their Messiah are in fact wrong and still, 'dead in their trespasses and sins,' Eph. 2:1; I Cor. 15:17. The answer is not found in sectarian name calling but: 1 - In a rational examination of the Biblical text; 2 - In the history of its interpretation; 3 - In it's relation to other Messianic prophecies whose Messianic meaning is beyond dispute. (All 333 or 456 of them!)

In Isaiah 52:13-15 you see in capsule form what Isaiah 53 contains; "The Servant" greatly exalted after being deeply humiliated. However, here in Isaiah 53:1-3 we draw some 'Principles for Living' from the 'Servant Despised' and the first thing we note in verse one is; **"The Challenge to Believe,"** and this opening statement is very strong in the Hebrew language! In fact that could have been our title for this section, "The Challenge To Believe!"

However, this verse lies in close connection to the previous verse, Isa. 52:15b, "For what had not been told them they shall see, and what they had not heard they shall consider." Remember verse divisions were added by Robert Stephanus a printer in 1551 and chapter divisions were added by Stephen Langton an archbishop of Canterbury in 1205. Before that it was just a continuous scroll, of continuous handwritten script. Based upon that, the Jewish people are introduced in Isa. 53:1 by saying, "Who has believed our report, or 'Who has believed what we have heard?" "And to whom is the arm of the LORD revealed?" (Or to whom has it been made plain, that the LORD sent His Servant/Son and had a hand in, all that He was and did for you.)

So, Isa.53:1 appears as an exclamation with what is to follow in vv. 2-12 and marks a contrast between those that heard and believed the revelation made in Isa. 52:15 and those that did not believe the revelation even though it was theirs to hear, believe and embrace. Isa. 53:1 states, "Who has believed our report?" (What we have heard; or, the thing heard by us).

Paul comments on this concept in Romans 10:16-17, "But they have not all obeyed the gospel. For Isaiah said, Lord, who has believed our report? So, then faith comes by hearing, and hearing by the word of God." Two reasons are given why 'ALL' ought to believe: 1 – The report of **'All'** the ancient prophets. 2 – The 'Arm of the LORD' exhibited in the Messiah while He was on the earth. (In fact if 'ALL' He did was recorded, John 21:25 says, "The world could not contain the books.") Or as one commentator put it, the penitent confession of the Jewish people will be, ***"How few of our nation in Messiah's days, believed in Him."***

"Who has believed our report?" However, in both Septuagint's, Thomson's and Brenton's this verse started with, "**O Lord,** who has believed our report?" This is also seen in Rom. 10:16 where it is quoted by Paul. What happened to,"O Lord?" Why was the *YHVH* dropped? It would change a prayer into a rhetorical question, but we will leave that for the critics.

Let me say something about the Greek Septuagint LXX. It is not a rival to the Hebrew manuscripts but a handmaiden, a pleasing asset to the house of God. It is not a choice, one or the other, Hebrew vs Greek. They are twin sisters, handmaidens of God's Word. The early church was made up of Greek speaking Jews, Hellenistic Jews. Acts 6, the deacons were appointed to care for the Hellenistic Jewish widows, check it out! Remember Egypt was a shelter for the Christ child from that neurotic king Herod and a storehouse for the written word of God. The largest library in the world was in Alexandria and around 250 BCE the Hebrew Scriptures were put into the Greek language of which there are many stories about how it came to be. The Jewish scholars were led to inscribe a record of the 'man of sorrows' in the heart of their treasured scriptures which they could never recant and 300 years later it was too late to deny the likeness to *Yeshua/Jesus* of Nazareth. Just a cursory reading of Isaiah 53 would easily prove the point!

The emphasis in this verse is on Israel's unbelief! Not necessarily on those who just heard, but on those who failed to believe. Only a remnant would believe and only a very small remnant at that! Isa. 1:9 states, "Except the LORD of hosts had left unto us <u>a very small remnant</u>, we should have been like Sodom, and we should have been like unto Gomorrah." (a tithe; a holy stump, a (*mat-seveth*) Isa. 6:13).

Isaiah is also calling attention to the world's lack of faith in general. This is more of an exclamation than an interrogative! Isaiah is speaking for all the prophets, not just for himself, 'Our Report!' (plural) The message or report is that, the Jewish Messiah would suffer and die. A horrible death, one you could date history by. This is the first time in all of the Scriptures that this was taught: "Israel's Messiah was going to suffer and die a horrible death!" One you could date history by.

The word report is the Hebrew word (*semua*) and means something heard, an announcement, a doctrine, a report, news or tidings. This word in Hebrew literally means, 'that which we have heard' or 'our message' what message? Remember the Ethiopian eunuch or treasurer in Acts 8:26-39 who was returning from Jerusalem reading a scroll. What was he reading when Philip ran up to his chariot? Isaiah 53:7-8, and if you check the Septuagint LXX it is almost word for word identical and Philip began right there and preached unto Him Jesus, read it for yourself! It also refers to the cumulative witness of all the prophets who for generations prophesied of a coming Savior to deliver His people from their sin. The reply to this rhetorical question is, 'Not Many!'

However, it raises an exegetical question, awaiting an answer! The words, 'Our report' simply means, 'The thing heard,' but is it a message we have heard or is it a message we proclaim? Most scholars take the later and translate it 'Our Preaching' and it fits much better into the context. This is also seen in the Newer Testament in John 12:37-48 and especially in Romans 10:14-21 ® So it is, "Who has believed our preaching?" Answer, very few!

In v.1 we see the Servant or the Messiah who alone, can atone for our sin. His **message** is rejected in v.1; His **person** is rejected in v.2; and His **mission** is rejected in v.3. However, His sufferings in v.4-6; His death & burial in v. 7-9; and His exaltation in v. 10-12, provide the atonement for all of our sins, which we shall also see. To miss the fact that the Servant of the LORD is our Messiah, the central figure in this passage is to stumble in unbelief over the cornerstone and the foundation of the good news seen Isaiah 52:7, "How beautiful upon the mountains are the feet of him <u>that brings good tidings, that publishes peace; that brings good tidings of good, that publishes salvation, that says unto Zion, Thy God reigns!</u>"

"And to whom is the arm of the LORD revealed?" The word revealed (*galah*) means to denude, to strip, to be bare naked. The word arm is (*zeroah*) and is the arm stretched out, meaning force, power and strength. It can also be the foreleg of an animal. *Zeroah* is the shank bone of a lamb on a 'Passover Plate.' Who are the only people, who have a shank bone on a plate every year for a celebration? The nation of Israel!

So, we have the bare arm of the LORD, an emblem of God's power, 'Always' connected with salvation, Always! For His people Israel and for the nations, the Gentiles, the Goi'im! When God made the universe He used His fingers Ps. 8:3, "When I consider the heavens, the work of Thy fingers…" When God delivered Israel out of Egypt He used His strong hand Ex. 13:3, "For by strength of hand, He brought you out of Egypt…" But to save a lost hell-bound world He had to strip bare His mighty arm Isa. 53:1 & 12, "The LORD made bare His holy arm in the eyes of all the nations…" Yet, so many fail to believe the demonstration of God's mighty power, read John 12:37-40.

In the Newer Testament the Gospel of God itself is the 'Power of God' unto salvation, Rom. 1:16. The LORD rolled up His sleeves and revealed His bare, 'naked arm' of salvation to the world! In Isa. 52:10 we see the Lord's arm in more detail and in its ultimate purpose, "The LORD has <u>made bare</u> His holy arm in the eyes of all the nations, and all the ends of the earth shall see the salvation of our God." (**all the nations**) (**all the ends of the earth**) (**shall see the salvation** - *the Yeshua of our God*).

I have been told by Rabbi's that nowhere in the Older Testament is the word salvation (*Yeshua*) ever used of a person. Really, turn to Isa. 62:11 and read it, "Behold, the LORD has proclaimed unto the end of the earth; Say ye to the daughter of Zion, Behold thy salvation (***thy Yeshua***) cometh; behold, **his** reward is with **him**, and **his** work before **him**." (I guess in that verse it is a real person!) I was sharing this with a man once, who was married to an Egyptian woman who had an Arabic translation and she said, "Look my Bible says, **"Here comes your Savior!"**

"The Arm of The LORD!" One of the keys to interpreting Isaiah 53 is the phrase **"The arm of the LORD"** and it is extremely important! Rabbi Alexander Harkavy said, "This phrase, "The Arm of the LORD" is used throughout the Scriptures to signify God's personal intervention in

Jewish history and particularly in the book of Isaiah, where it is used as a name for the promised Messiah."

Isaiah uses it over ten times from Isa. 33:2 where He reigns over Israel in peace to Isa. 63:5 where He delivers Israel out of *Bozrah/Petra* at the end of, 'Jacob's Trouble' with His garments red with blood. In Isaiah 40, God foretells a visit which He Himself will make to planet earth for the sole purpose of cleansing Israel of their sins. Isa. 40:2 Isaiah says, "Speak ye tenderly to Jerusalem, and cry unto her, that her warfare is accomplished, that her iniquity is pardoned; for she has received of the LORD's hand double (*kep-layim- kepel* in the plural tense, or a double doubling) for all her sins." (Quadruple!) Isa. 40:3 goes on to say, "The voice of him that cries in the wilderness, **Prepare ye the way of the LORD, make straight** in the desert **a highway for our God**." Why would you have to do that? Because He was coming for a visit, that's why!

Again in Isaiah 51:5 the **LORD's arm** is seen as the instrument of His deliverance from evil; "My righteousness is near; My salvation is gone forth, and **Mine arms** shall judge the peoples; the isles shall wait upon Me, and in/on **Mine arm** shall they trust." Then again to His promise Israel cries out in Isa. 51:9, "Awake, awake, put on strength, **O arm of the LORD**; awake, as in the ancient days, in the generations of old. Was it not thou, who hast cut Rahab and wounded the dragon?"

It is clear by the time we get to Isaiah 52 that God is speaking about an act of deliverance and cleansing which He Himself is going to perform through His **'Holy Arm,'** in Isa. 52:10; "The LORD has made bare His **'Holy Arm'** in the eyes of all the nations; and all the ends of the earth shall see the salvation (*the Yeshua*) of our God." There is quite a contrast between 'The arm of the LORD' in v.1 which speaks of power; and 'The root out of a dry ground' in v.2 which speaks of humility and meekness, not weakness-meekness. (In fact where does a mighty oak get its nourishment, strength and growth from? Its roots, in fact if a tree does not have a good root system it will topple over in a storm and die!)

Ps. 1:3 says, "And he shall be like a tree planted by the rivers of water, that brings forth its fruit in its season; its leaf also shall not wither and whatsoever he does shall prosper." A tree has three priorities: 1 – **First** it has to draw **enough** nutrients and water out of the ground to stay alive; 2

– **Second** it has to draw **extra** nutrients out of the ground and water to promote growth; 3 – **Third** it has to draw **excess** nutrients and water out of the ground to produce fruit. So, fruit is simply, excess life! (Think about that the next time you are eating a piece of fruit, you are simply eating excess life!) The same thing is true of 'Believers and the Bible' are you getting enough to stay alive, are you getting extra to promote growth, and are you getting some excess to produce fruit?

An outline of Isaiah 52 may help to bring the figure of God's promised Messiah into focus and serve as an introduction to this controversial chapter, Isaiah 53, **'The Crown Jewel'** of the Older Testament; Isaiah 52: v.1-6 is, **The call to holiness**; v.7-8 is, **The promise of the One who will bring 'Good Tidings;'** v.9-10 is, **God's salvation to be manifested in His 'Holy Arm;'** v.11-12 is, **The second call to holiness**; and v.13-15 is, **The suffering Servant whose blood shall sprinkle many nations**. You see it's in this wider context of Israel's need for cleansing and God's promise for a sin-bearing Servant that Isaiah 53 must be understood.

Isa. 59:16 says, "And he saw that there was no man, and wondered that there was no intercessor; therefore, his arm brought salvation unto him, and his righteousness sustained him." (Ezk. 22:20). The **'Arm of the LORD'** is Israel's Messiah, who brings salvation to what, Isa. 52:10, all the nations and all the ends of the earth, not just Israel, all the nations of the earth!

Interesting, they executed *Yeshua*/Jesus stark naked before the whole world, between two criminals, and buried him in a rich man's tomb, "And they made his grave with the wicked, And with the rich his tomb," Isa. 53:9a, JPS translation, 1917. As my favorite Rabbi says, "Coincidence is not a kosher word." You can see this in more detail as you study, Isa. 53:12.

"Christian scholars" says, Isaac Abravanel/Abarbanel, "interpret Isaiah 53 as referring to 'that man' who was crucified in Jerusalem about the end of the Second Temple and who according to their view was the Son of God who became a man in the womb of a Virgin. Jonathan ben Uziel explains it as the Messiah who has yet to come and this is the opinion of the ancients in many of the Midrashim."

So, even the synagogue and its leaders could not help acknowledging that this passage is about their Messiah, predicting His death and glory and it is not referring to Israel. What is needed is Daniel 9:24-27 to set the date of the Messiah's coming before the Temple's destruction in 70 AD. Dan. 9 tells you when & where to look for the Messiah; Isa. 53 tells you who & what to look for in a Messiah; together they are like a birthday invitation, so you don't miss Him! A short verse in Hebrew, only seven words and in English 15 yet it sets the bar for 'The Crown Jewel' of the Older Testament which you are about to study.

Lord, help us to read between the lines and to search your word diligently, for the truth that leads to eternal life. Or as our Jewish friends pray, 'Blessed art Thou O Lord our God, King of the universe, Who has given us the Torah of truth and life eternal implanted within us.' Help us O Lord as we search Your word for truth, understanding and life, in the name of the blessed *Mashiach, ha Shem, Yeshua,* we pray. Amen!

****

Part Two: The Servant's Roots Matured – Isa. 53:2

Blaise Pascal a Christian philosopher, writer, mathematician, physicist, and child prodigy stated, "If the entire 'Physical Universe' conspired to crush a man, the man would still be nobler than the entire 'Physical Universe,' because he would know that he was crushed." (You will have to read that several times, I had to!) In other words, he has something the universe doesn't 'knowledge.' It is this personal self-consciousness, this knowledge, that makes the human nature infinitely great, and we find in this human nature its highest level raised in the infinite God-man, since He is to become the object of our worship and win us to Himself. Apart from the revelation of Jesus Christ we have no sure knowledge of God other than an impersonal force, like other religions (Buddhism, Judaism, Islam, etc) Jn. 10:30; 14:9; Heb. 1:3.

If you take Christ out of Christianity it vanishes before your very eyes into intellectual vapor, and is non-existent without the Messiah, the 'Suffering Servant' in this passage! The hyphen, that little dash, never means more than when it appears between the words, 'God-Man.' It both connects and separates, He is as much God as though He is not man and as much man as though He is not God. He is God's perfect man and man's perfect God! He is the infinite, incarnate, immutable, omnificent Servant/Messiah of the Most High God!

Men of Isaiah's day, as well as men today look upon the pathetic idea of a 'Suffering Servant' as not very credible, because it is not humanly possible to reconcile greatness with suffering. When people prosper we say, "They must be living right." When the opposite happens we have a tendency to say, "What's wrong in your life, Job?" (When neither evaluation is entirely correct). As someone once said, "A Servant or Messiah without earthly splendor; humble, humiliated tormented; who dies on a shameful cross as a vicarious, voluntary sacrifice, for the redemption of Israel and all mankind, has always been and still remains an offense to Jewish thinking!"

In Isa. 53:2, the word grow is the Hebrew word (*alah*) to ascend, mount, be high, to rise, to spring or shoot up. It is referring to normal growth, not a sudden dazzling visit as expected by the Jewish people. This Servant or Messiah was born a King but He was born to poor, peasant parents. The 'Wise Men' came asking, "Where is he that has been born, King of the Jews?"

No one is born a King, you could be born a prince, and become a King, but Israel's Messiah would assume King David's throne and He would be born a King. In fact this became a stumbling block to the Jewish leaders in, Matt. 13:53-58. That's the reason for rejecting of their Messiah, He wasn't exactly what they were expecting. They were looking for a tall tree, a king on a white horse, not a tender plant on a donkey.

"For he shall grow up <u>before Him</u> (*YHWH*)..." (Not them! Note it, it is very important!) This would be better translated, 'He grew up before Him." This shows the force of the historical tense, all the verbs are past tense, and have completed action, until v.7. As one author put it, "All have been finished before the foundation of the world, in the Divine Counsels." Acts 2:22-23; Eph. 1:4, "He has chosen us in Him before the foundation of the world." It is prophetically spoken, of a future event as having been completed. God always looks at history as fact even though it may be 700 years in the future.

"Before Him..." (*pa-neh*) means before the face of Jehovah, before the (*YHWH*), before the great 'I AM' under the scrutiny of the watchful eye of 'Almighty God,' *El Shaddai* and in conformity to His perfect will and purpose. (What would the world know of His growing up?) Nothing! <u>Absolutely Nothing</u>! In the Newer Testament it states regarding *Yeshua*/Jesus, "The child grew and became strong in spirit, filled with wisdom, and the grace of God was upon him. And *He* increased in wisdom and stature and in favor **with God** and man." Luke 2:40; 52.

Yet "...like a tender plant..." Like a (*yo-neq*) a suckling, a twig, a sprout or a stalk indicating a young sapling. The root of this word means to nurse or to 'suck' hence the word suckling, from which we get the English term 'sucker' which is applied to horticulture. So, Isaiah is thinking of a 'shoot' or 'sucker' from the stump of a tree that was recently cut down.

Earlier he had spoken of the Servant/Messiah as a 'shoot' from the stump of Jesse in Isa. 11:1. A tree cut off at ground level will produce shoots from its roots! Therefore, He is to grow up like a 'sucker' from a dead tree stump. The tree is dead but not the stump or the roots. There is still life under the surface.

The term, "like a tender plant" indicates 'Servant-Hood' and vulnerability. A young shoot can be broken, crushed, scorched, stepped on, or even eaten up by an animal. The connection between the Messiah proclaimed in the first part of Isaiah and the Suffering Servant of God in the second part of Isaiah is very obvious to the student of the Scriptures. The J.P.S. translation of 1955 translates Isa. 11:1, "And there shall come forth a shoot out of the stock of Jesse, And a twig shall grow forth out of his roots." (The phrase, 'the root of Jesse' is a Messianic title).

"...and like a root (*sores*) out of a dry ground;" (*eretz tziah*) A root out of a dry-ground recalls the fact that God's plants spring up and grow in the most unlikely places. A parched, arid, barren, dry, waterless, desert. Interesting, Zion means (dry-spot). I think there is more of a miraculous, supernatural growth here then meets the eye. Dry ground is not lush soil or fertile ground! In fact it is anything but that!

A young, tender, sprout wouldn't make it one day, stuck in a hot, arid, scorching, desert. There is quite a contrast between the 'arm of the

LORD' in v.1 showing God's almighty power and a 'root out of a dry ground' in v.2 showing humiliation and meekness, not weakness. ("The meek shall inherit the earth," Matt. 5:5). The term 'tender plant' indicates his Servant-hood; Remember they were looking for a tall tree (a king) not a tender plant (a servant). "A root out of a dry ground" also points to 'His Deity' indicating the miraculous and the supernatural. King Herod tried to completely wipe out the Davidic blood line! TRIED! & Died! In 4 B.C.

The burning bush was fueled supernaturally and this tender plant would also have to be nourished supernaturally, not from the parched ground, but from above! (*ano-then*) Just like *Yeshua*/Jesus said to Nicodemus in John 3:3, he had to be born-again, 'Born from above' (*ano-then*) spiritually, supernaturally! They were looking for the natural, a man to deliver them not the supernatural, not for God to deliver them. Too bad, they missed their special delivery that night!

There are three types of plants familiar to a gardener: A hardy native plant, almost impossible to kill; The half-hardy plant that adapts to its environment; you can kill it if you try real hard; The exotic, tender plant that finds its environment, extremely hostile to life and it's almost impossible to keep alive. (That is the metaphor for our, 'Tender Plant' in v.2).

Isaiah uses the same metaphor in 11:1, "And there shall come forth a rod (*koter* – switch, shoot, twig) out of the stem (*geza* – stump, root stock) of Jesse, and a Branch (*Netzer* – shoot of a plant) shall grow out of his roots (*sores* – root, bottom, base of a plant, source of a family line);" How beautiful is that? A shoot shall come out of the stump of Jesse and a Branch shall grow out of his base or family line.

The phrase, "...a root out of a dry ground;" Has four possibilities: To Israel degraded, enslaved, downtrodden, suppressed, over taxed, and beaten: To the virgin birth, a barren, unfertilized womb, of a young, betrothed, Jewish maiden: To the dead spiritual life of Israel and its forgotten people: To an ancient decayed family, but in whose roots there was still **HOPE** and life, a shoot, a sprout. **(Or all four!)** (Israel's National Anthem is "*Ha Tikvah* – The Hope!)

As stated the terms 'Tender Shoot' and 'Root' have Messianic connotations both in Scripture and in Rabbinic literature, and Isaiah is employing them both in this Servant. In fact, in the prophetic writings the Messiah is often called a "Root" or a "Branch" as in Isaiah 11 where the Shoot's role parallels that of the Servant's in Isa. 53. "And there shall come forth a rod out of the stem of Jesse, and a **Branch** shall grow out of his **roots**." (In both passages Isa. 11 & 53 Jehovah is appointing a leader to bring about change in the land and in the people).

Isaiah 11:10 says, "And in that day there shall be a **Root** of Jesse, who shall stand for an ensign of the peoples; to him shall the Gentiles seek, and his rest shall be glorious." You have four characteristics describing the Servant/Messiah as **The Branch**:

1 - You have the, "**The Branch of the LORD**," Isa. 4:2 says, "In that day shall the Branch of the LORD be beautiful and glorious and the fruit of the earth shall be excellent…" Isa.7:14; Matt. 25:31.

2 - You have the, "**The Branch of David**," Jer. 23:5 says, "Behold the days come says the LORD, that I will raise unto David a righteous Branch and a King.." Isa. 11:1; Jer. 33:15; Rom. 1:3

3 - You have the, "**The LORD's Servant the Branch**," Zech. 3:8 says, "For behold I will bring forth My servant the Branch." Isa. 52:13-15; and 53:1-12; Phil. 2:5-8;

4 - You have the, "**Man whose name is The Branch**," Zech. 6:12 says, "Behold the Man whose name is the Branch…" that is, his character as the Son of man, the last Adam. I Cor. 15:45-47.

Each one of these references is showing a different character of the Servant/Messiah; 1- Immanuel, in His birth; 2 - Messiah - King of kings, in His life; 3 – Humiliation, in His death; 4 - The Son of man, in His kingdom, reigning as 'Priest-King' over the earth.

In the Newer Testament: Matthew is the Gospel of the **Branch** of David; Mark is the Gospel of the Lord's Servant, the **Branch**; Luke is the Gospel, of the Man whose name is the **Branch**; and John is the Gospel of the **Branch** of the Lord. (See, C.I. Scofield's note; on Isa. 4:2) Isaiah 11 involves Jehovah bringing the people back and making them at peace with one another; Isaiah 53 involves Jehovah bearing the iniquities of the people in v.12, through the *(asham,* guilt or trespass offering) in v.10. As I said earlier in both passages He is appointing a leader to bring about change in the land and in the people. *Yeshua/Jesus* Himself claims this title in Rev. 22:16 in the last message of the Bible in the new heaven and the new earth, "I am the root and the offspring of David, the bright and the morning star."

"He has no form, nor comeliness..." He has 'No' *(to-ar)* no outward beauty, no fair countenance, no majestic kingliness to attract human admiration. Nor comeliness *(ha-dar)* nor magnificence, nor splendor, nor glory! In other words there was nothing extraordinary about His outward appearance! Nothing that would cause us to desire or delight in him or greatly love him. There was no outward beauty, no splendor, no glory, no good looks, no handsomeness! Just a plain, ordinary man in a robe with sandals and a beard; 'Just plain vanilla, no sprinkles!' The question Nathaniel asked was, "Can any good thing come out of Nazareth?" John 1:46. Pretty conclusive, pretty comprehensive, pretty concrete, but not the final word, not yet anyway!

"And when we shall see Him, there is no beauty that we should desire Him." His appearance was not designed to attract the natural man. There is a difference between glamour and glory! There was nothing to attract the eye and hold its attention. Nothing! In other words, "the form of beauty" they sought was not holiness, but military might and personal glory. A strong man, a mighty man, a military leader to destroy the Romans!

Can you recall the crowd's cry when Pilate brought Him out, "Not this man, but Barabbas!" John 18:40. They wanted a revolutionary, someone who could fight their battles, not forgive their sins! The world waits for a 'Military Messiah' now to lead them into political, religious and cultural supremacy, a 'King Saul,' not a 'King Jesus' and they are about to get their wish! The Anti-Christ may be on the scene and growing in popularity and strength right now!

Humility, holiness, the cross, a 'Suffering Servant' are all a scandal to this unregenerate world we live in, Jewish and Gentile, except to blood bought, born-again Christians. However, they forget political restoration to supremacy is founded on 'Spiritual Regeneration' as pictured in Ezek. 37

and, 'The Vision of The Dry Bones," and that demanded the incarnation and the personal atonement of Israel's Servant/Messiah.

Note the masculine, singular, personal, pronouns in this verse pointing to the Servant, "**He** shall grow up...**He** has no form...we shall see **Him**...we should desire **Him**." If the Servant is Israel, as Jewish people claim, who is the 'We' (plural) included with the prophet Isaiah, in v.2?

The natural mind is all too ready to interpret meekness for weakness and to waste its praise on the proud, pompous, self-seeking class. However, His appearance was like that of a stunted shrub, struggling to survive in arid soil, gasping for breath and grasping for His Father's hand! (Psalm 22).

"There is no beauty *(mar-eh)* that we should desire Him..." This speaks of the despicable almost universal judgment of this world, except for those whom *El Shaddai* has drawn toward His Beloved, through His grace. The true beauty of this Servant was portrayed in His suffering and His majesty was displayed in His humility, as seen in the life of *Yeshua/Jesus*. How is your portrait unveiled before God? The spiritual beauties of holy sweet communion can only be recognized if spiritually discerned. "The eye admires only what the heart truly can see."

The world wants a 'Sovereign Ruler' they have to pay tax to, not a 'Suffering Savior' they have to pay homage to. How strange and twisted man's mind has become over time. Though Jesus Christ arose from the dead, the Jewish people regarded Him as a person who had been crucified, disgraced and they rejected and despised him as the offscouring of the earth.

Yet the Scriptures are very clear, "Every knee shall bow, and every tongue confess, that *Yeshua ha Maschiach,* Jesus the Christ, is Lord, to the glory of God the Father. "Every Tongue and Every Knee" on earth, in heaven and under the earth, shall bow and shall confess! Phil. 2:9-11. Why wait until you are forced to bow and hear those wretched words, "Depart form Me, for I never knew you!" Why not call out to Him today and receive this 'Servant/Messiah' as your 'Lord & Savior' and then you will hear those blessed words, "Enter thou into the joy of the Lord." Three words from your heart to the heart of God (if you mean them) will do it, "Lord, Save, Me!"

PRAYER - "Father, it is hard for us to understand Your will, Your plan, Your counsel sometimes but our part is to just trust You and lean not unto our own understanding. Because sometimes our commonsense makes no sense and leads to nonsense. So please Father, give more to us faith today, to trust You more and ourselves less. We don't have to understand Your Word, we just have to read it and heed it because we need it. In Your Son's name, in *ha Shem Yeshua* we pray! Amen!

****

Part Three: The Servant's Sorrow Unveiled – Isa. 53:3

We could have entitled this, "The Reception of The Servant!" or "The Rejection of The Servant!" In this verse we have the pure, unadulterated aversion of the Jewish nation toward Jehovah's Servant. Isaiah the prophet uses a series of verbs to provide a detailed description of the intense suffering of the assumed subject, Jehovah's Servant, and His whole life would be characterized by suffering not royalty. "He was despised, and forsaken of men, A man of pains, and acquainted with disease, And as one from whom men hide their face: He was despised, and we esteemed him not." J.P.S. Trans. 1966. I don't know about you, but that sounds like a person not a nation to me, so let's take a closer look at this verse.

"He is despised..." To despise (*ba-zah*) means to disdain, scorn, to be contemptible; Franz Delitzsch says, "Despised connotes, bitter contempt and is translated 'vile person' in other places, referring to the most hated man in Jewish history, 'Antiochus Epiphanies' who is set forth as the foreshadow of the antichrist and the most hated person in all of Jewish history. Mr. Nasty, that's who they compare Him too. Many Jewish people hate *Yeshua/Jesus* more than Satan himself. This gives you a slight glimpse into the Jewish feeling for *Yeshua/Jesus.*

Twice this word despised (*ba-zah*) is used in v.3 to emphasize its intensity and severity. "He is despised" - present tense! "He was despised" - past tense! And, "He shall be despised" - future tense!

"And Rejected of men..." He was rejected (*chadal*) abandoned, refused, forsaken, but not forgotten, to be destitute, to desist or cease to exist. John 1:11 says, "He came unto His own, and His own received Him not!" By not accepting or receiving someone, you are in fact rejecting or refusing Him. 'Rejected of men;' Jews, Gentiles, Rich, Poor, Rank, Great, Learned, Religious, etc; (*ish-im, men of nobility*). No prophecy was ever more strikingly fulfilled than that one, **"Rejected of men!"** (let that sink in!)

The Hebrew name for Jesus - *Yeshua/Savior* has been deliberately distorted to **"Yeshu"** *(no 'a' not Yeshua – note it!)* **or "Isschu"** an acronym for **"Immach Schemo Vezikro!"** **The letters of "Yeshu or Isschu" spell out a sentence, "Let his name and memory be blotted out forever." (Forgotten, Destitute, Forsaken)**. Don't let anyone use it on you! No name has aroused more antagonism and opposition among Jewish people than the name of 'Jesus Christ' who came to give His life a ransom for His people and the world. "No Name!"

This aversion to Him has even increased with the passing of time. His name is not even mentioned among Jewish people other than, 'that man' or 'the hanged one' or 'the illegitimate one' or in mockery or slang or as a cuss word. (It's amazing to me!) However, among many Reform and Conservative Jewish people, this attitude is gradually changing to a more positive attitude. (2,000 years and He is still intimidating people!)

Rejected by who? **MEN!** (*ish-im*) There are three words for man in Hebrew: (***enosh***) used of man in his weakness; (***adom***) used of man in general; and (***ish***) used of man in his strength and as nobility or lord's of people. This is true of the only other usages of (***ish-im***) in: Ps. 141:4 and Prov. 8:4. It is used of men of Rank, men of Stature, and men of Standing. The Leaders; The Elders; The Kings; We saw it in Isaiah 52:15, "kings shall shut their mouths at him." (Turn away in disgust!)

So, this Servant is going to be 'Rejected - (*chadal*) abandoned, refused, forsaken, by men of 'Rank and Prestige' with few exceptions like *Nicodemus* and Joseph of *Arimathaea*. Remember the words of the Jewish leaders in the N. T. in John 7:48, "Have any of the rulers or the Pharisees believed on Him?" Read I Cor. 1:26-29 sometime for God's view point!

Listen to the touching cry of Psalm 69:12, a prophecy of scornful discussions of the elders or leaders, "They that sit in the gate speak against me, and I was the song of the drunkards." The butt end of jokes? A cuss word in a conversation! Despicable! Contemptible! God is not damning anything yet!

The word 'against' is always used in Hebrew of a downward scorn. This is not a special few but it was universal. "The nations rejected him!" The fact that God said they would reject Him and the majority did reject Him is strong evidence for Who He is! Many who claim to revere Him today would also despise him if they knew what the Newer Testament really said about Him.

"A man of sorrows..." Note if you will the words; **"Men & Man"** *(ish-im & ish)* in this verse. Obviously if *(ishim)* is plural and is individual men, then *(ish)* is singular and must be an individual man and cannot, **(CANNOT)** be a nation! "A man of sorrows *(mak'oboth)* severe pains, plural. This is a **man** whose chief distinction was, that His life was one of constant, painful, afflictions which could either be physical or spiritual or both!

What a contrast to Isaiah 52:13, "Behold, My Servant...exalted, extolled and elevated..." The root word for sorrows is to feel pain, to agonize, and to suffer torment. Isa. 9:6 says, "For unto us a child was born…" showing His humanity, the Son of man; and "Unto us a Son was given…" showing His deity, the Son of God. He had to be both 'God and man' to pay the ultimate sacrifice and atone for man's sin. It is impossible for a sinful man to redeem his fellow man, read Psalm 49:7-8.

Yeshua/Jesus said in Matt. 26:38, "My soul is exceedingly sorrowful, even unto death." He agonized in the garden; He sweat great drops of blood, *(hematohidrosis)*. Lk. 22:44. He wept strong *(ischyros –* mighty, powerful, forceful) tears. Heb. 5:7. He cried for the cup to pass three times; He felt the bitterness of betrayal; He was tried by the people He came to save; He was crowned with two inch thorns; He was scourged with a cat of nine tails by the Romans, and hung on a cross naked. He was forsaken by God and His disciples and His heart ruptured from His sufferings.

The Servant came to suffer with and for His people and to lay down His life for them. Such were the facts of history and the prophetic requirements of Scripture were fulfilled. The Messiahship was proven; and satisfaction for sin was made, Isaiah 53:11, "He (God) shall see the travail of his soul and shall be satisfied (*saba*)." Sounds like an (onomatopoeia) a word that is spelled like the sound it makes, like ahhh!

"And acquainted with grief..." *(Or sickness)*. Not that He was diseased with viruses or bacteria but that the wrath instigated by sin and the zeal of self-sacrifice burned within Him like a fever. Psalm 69:9-10 says, "For the zeal of thine house has eaten me up; and the reproaches of those who reproached thee are fallen on me." We are not talking about physical sickness here, these are the result of sin and this Servant was absolutely sinless, perfect, without spot or blemish!

What is implied here is that the wrath of Almighty God instigated by sin was poured out upon His Servant. The word for 'grief or sickness' stands for, 'SIN!' Isaiah uses this same figure in Isaiah 1:4-6, read it. He drank that bitter cup of God's wrath to the very dregs after thanking Him for it and then He climbed up on our cross and was made SIN for you and for me. II Cor. 5:21. That's why He cried from the tree, *("Eli, Eli lama sabachthani,")* "My God, My God why have You forsaken Me?" Ps. 22:1 Hab. 1:13; Why? Ps. 22:3, "Thou art Holy," (*kodosh*, sacred, pure). He is Holy and Holiness demands Holiness!

This word can be translated sickness, disease, anxiety, affliction, but the context will determine the proper translation, not the translator's opinion. Many suppose the figure is 'Leprosy' the most severe sickness known to man at that time and many times imposed by God on man. The ancient Rabbis refer to this Servant as one who was shunned like a Leper.

The word 'acquainted' (*yada*) means to know intimately by personal experience. Adam (*yada'd*) knew, Eve and she conceived, that's personal, and that's intimate! Gen. 4:1. The word literally means, 'Introduced!' Messiah meet pain, grief, sorrow, torment, SIN! Pain, grief, sorrow, torment, SIN meet the Messiah! To become 'acquainted' with is the same thing in Hebrew (*yada*) means to become intimate with it.

Listen, we endure pain, we tolerate grief and sorrow, we put up with it, we don't become intimate with it, do we? He did, and He did it for you and for me! He embraced it, all His life! That's why the Jewish people in John 8:57 said of *Yeshua/Jesus*, "Thou art not yet fifty years old and hast

Thou seen Abraham?" (Look at pictures of our presidents before and after four years and see how they have aged).

He was never seen to laugh, and was so worn away from continual grief, that when He was in His mid thirties he was taken to be nearly 50 years of age, John 8:57. How? From being "acquainted (*yada*) with the grief," of the world and bearing that burden all of His life. We never read that He laughed, but we often read that He wept, John 11:35 at the tomb of Lazarus; At Jerusalem upon His triumphal entry, Luke 19:41; In Gethsemane before going to the cross, Heb. 5:7. (So, I guess grown men do cry!)

"And we (plural) hid as it were our (plural) faces from Him (sing)..." He was like a thing or person from which a man turns away his face in shame or disgust! Isaiah 49:7 says, "Thus saith the LORD, the Redeemer of Israel, and his Holy One, to him whom man despiseth (*bazah*) to him whom the nation abhorreth (*ta-ab* - to loathe, detest, to be abominable) to a servant of rulers;" The natural mind is all to ready to construe meekness for weakness and to waste its praise on the proud and the self-seeking.

There are several thoughts and possibilities on this phrase. They turned away their faces from Him in horror; They had to turn from the suffering; They turned from Him in contempt; They turned away from Him in scorn because He was so unlike what they expected and they hid their faces in real contempt.

But you never hide your face, your testimony, your convictions from Him, do you? You never turn away? You never keep silent when you know a word or testimony must be spoken? You always stand up for Christ and His children, and do the right thing, right?

"He was despised (*bazah*) and we esteemed (*chasab*) Him not." Now we hit the bottom of the pit with this dreary repetition; "So, we despised Him and deemed Him insignificant and unimportant." We did not reckon Him and we did not evaluate Him properly. Some refer to Him as, "Less than a man;" others as, "The most abject of men." (Lit. – He who ceases from men, that is, 'Is no longer regarded as a man.' Hengstenberg, Ps. 49:7)

So, it is with the human race, they acknowledge but do not evaluate Him correctly. Luther said, "We estimated Him as nothing!" *'NOTHING!'* "They made *Him* like the off-scouring and refuge in the midst of the people." Lam. 3:45. Ps. 69:12 says, "I am the songs of the drunkards." Nothing more than spiritual derision and scum. People loathe to look at a man whom they hate immensely. In all of the history of Israel no one was more intensely hated or despised than this 'Servant of God.' **"NO ONE!"**

"We (plural) hid our faces from Him." We shunned Him like a leper; we turned away in contempt, and scorn. He was abandoned, abhorred, a reproach of men, a worm and no man, and the off-scouring of the earth. Why? Luke 19:14, "We will not have this man to reign over us!" The word means, 'to have an aversion to someone or something.' Psalm 22:6-8, "But I am a worm (*towla*) and no man; a reproach of men, and despised by the people. All they who see Me laugh Me to scorn; they shoot out the lip, they shake the head saying, He trusted in the LORD that He would deliver Him; let Him deliver Him, seeing He delighted in Him." (Matt. 27:39-44)

We did not reckon Him! We did not value Him! We did not esteem Him! We did not elevate Him! Who is the 'WE' in v.3? It must be the Nation of Israel, but it does not exclude the *Goi'im!* Who can estimate the guilt of the self-righteous religious leaders who sneer at the precious blood of our Servant, our Messiah and tear it from their Hymnals, Scriptures, and Bibles today? There is a lesson for us to learn from all this. Why should we seek the approval of a world which despises our LORD? Or why should we desire acceptance from men who reject Him?

So, it is with the whole human race today, they acknowledge the Servant the Messiah but; They don't value Him; They esteem Him correctly! A good man, a prophet, a teacher, but not the Messiah, not the Savior of mankind. We must bring Him down to our level they say, "He is a man just like us and He would probably flunk mathematics." Or as one writer put it, "We estimated him as nothing!" (How can they do that?)

Listen to Ps. 69:12 one more time, "They that sit in the gate (The Leaders) speak against Me, and I was the songs of the drunkards." Is that all He is, this Servant, this Messiah? The song of drunkards, the topic of scorn, a derogatory remark or joke, an occasional cuss word when something goes wrong, or when you slam your finger in the door? Nothing more than a cuss word in a book or in a movie! No offense meant!

You say, 'I have never despised Him, I have never rejected Him, I have never shunned Him, I have never turned my back on Him, I have never not exalted Him! **Really Peter!** Though all those others forsake Him, you never will! Why, you will even die for Him, Right! Listen, this Servant, this Messiah, *Yeshua/Jesus* doesn't want you to die for Him; He wants you to live for Him, one day at a time, starting right now! That begins by giving up the 'Right to yourself!'

Peter denied Him three times and he was only 30 feet away from Him when he did it, a stone's throw, and their eyes met and he turned as it were and "hid his face from him in shame." In fact Peter denied the Faith, he denied the Brotherhood and he denied the Lord. Matt. 26:69-75; and Mark 22:54-62. But don't be too quick to judge Peter, how many times does the 'Cock Crow' every day in your life or mine? In John 21, *Yeshua/Jesus* restored Peter three times! We may not reject Him! We may not despise Him! But do we shun Him or turn our back on Him when we pick up that magazine in the drug store, watch an 'R' rated movie or worse, the internet, or listen to an off color joke or music?

Do you Exalt Him, Extol Him, Elevate Him in all your conversations and business deals? Do you esteem Him in every area of your life, thoughts, words, deeds, taxes? He died for you, so you could live for Him! He took your Hell so you could take His Heaven! He drank your cup, so you didn't have too! He took your sin, so you could take His righteousness! He took your whip, your nails, your thorns, your spit, your spear, your shame, your scorn; So you could have His love, His mercy, His grace, and His forgiveness!

What does it mean to suffer the infinite wrath of God? I don't know and I never will! Because He endured it for you and me, on a hill He made, on a tree He created, in a city His Father loves! "He was despised (*bazah*) became a vile person, and we esteemed Him not." (How Terrible!) All He did for you; All He left behind; All the glory He emptied Himself of; All the majesty He turned his back on; All the shame, the spitting, the beating, the cursing, the mocking, the loneliness, the pain, the sorrow, the nakedness, the grief, the sin, and ***'We Esteem Him Not!'***

Tell me, isn't it a shame, in light of the cross and all that He did for us on Calvary, that we live such defeated lives before Him? Be honest, are you living a victorious life for Christ? Can you answer Paul's question in the affirmative to the early church, "Are you saved, are you living the crucified life?" I Cor. 2:2. If not, why not?

****

Chapter Three: The Servant Wounded (Isa 53:4-6)

****

Part One: The Servant Afflicted Mercilessly – Isa. 53:4

The Third Stanza

This 'Crown Jewel' of the older Testament has captivated the hearts and minds of Bible students and scholars for centuries if not millenniums. Kyle Yates called it, "The Mt. Everest of the Old Testament;" Polycarp called it, "The Golden passional of the old testament evangelist;" and Spurgeon referred to it as, "The Bible in miniature and the Gospel in its essence."

It is comprised of five strophes of stanzas, of three verses each. Thus far we have examined: "The Servant Exalted" Isa. 52:13-15: and, "The Servant Despised" Isa. 53 1-3: Now we will begin to examine the third stanza, "The Servant Wounded" Isa. 53:4-6: then we will examine, "The Servant Cut-Off" Isa. 53:7-9: and "The Servant Satisfied" Isa. 53:10-12.

However, the third stanza Isaiah 53:4-6, "The Servant Wounded" presents the heart of the passage and the heart of the gospel, the innocent Servant dying as the sacrifice for sin. That very message lies at the very heart of Israel's religious system, an innocent sacrifice, dying for guilty sinners, Lev. 16. *Yeshua/Jesus* bore our sin on the tree on Calvary, I Pet. 2:24, but He also identified with the consequences of Adam's sin when He ministered to the people all around Him.

The emphasis in vv. 4-6 is on the plural pronouns: our griefs; our sorrows; our iniquities; our transgression; we have gone astray; we have turned to our own way. He did not die because of anything He had done, but because of what we had done. He was 'wounded' means 'pierced through.' His hands and feet were pierced with nails, Ps. 22:16; Lk. 24:39-40; and His side with a spear, John. 19:31-37; Zech. 12:10; Rev. 1:7. Crucifixion was not a Jewish form of execution, John 12:32-33; 18:31-32. Capital punishment to the Jewish people meant stoning, Lev. 24:14; Num. 15:35-36. If they wished to further humiliate their victim, they would just publicly expose the corpse longer, Deut. 21:22-23, a practice that Peter related to the Crucifixion, Acts 5:30; 10:39; I Pet. 2:24.

On the cross, *Yeshua/Jesus* was 'bruised' which means, "crushed under the weight of a burden." What was that burden? "The LORD laid on Him the iniquity of us all" Isa. 53:6, 12; Isa. 1:4. Sin is indeed a burden that grows heavier the longer we resist God, Ps. 38:4, "For mine iniquities are gone over mine head, like an heavy burden, they are too heavy for me."

He was "chastised" and given many "stripes" and yet that punishment brought us peace and healing. The only way a lawbreaker can be at peace with the law is to suffer the punishment that the law demands. *Yeshua/Jesus* kept the law perfectly, yet He suffered the whipping that belonged to us. Because He took our place, we now have peace with God and cannot be condemned by God's law, Rom. 5:1; 8:1. The "healing" in Isa. 53:5 refers to forgiveness of sins, not the healing of the body, I Pet. 2:24, "Who His own self bore our sins in His own body on the tree, that we being dead to sins, should live unto righteousness; by whose stripes you were healed." Sin is not only like a burden, but it is also like a sickness that only God can cure, Isa. 1:4-6; Jer. 30:12; Nah. 3:19.

Sin is serious business. The prophet calls it transgression, which means rebellion against God, daring to cross the line that God has drawn, Isa. 53:5, 8. He also calls it iniquity, which refers to the crookedness of our sinful nature, vv. 5-6. In other words, we are sinners by choice and by nature. Like sheep, we are born with a nature that prompts us to go astray and like sheep we foolishly decide to go our own way. By nature we are born children of wrath, Eph. 2:3, and by choice we become children of disobedience, Eph. 2:2.

Under God's Law, the good sheep died for the shepherd! Lev. 16

Under God's Grace, the Good Shepherd died for the sheep! John 10

In this strophe or stanza of three verses to be examined, lie one of the most graphic descriptions of the Servant's death in all the Scriptures; vv 4-6 should give us nightmares if not night sweats. In v. 4 – 'The Servant is Afflicted Mercilessly!' In v. 5 – 'The Servant is Wounded Fatally!' And in v.6 – 'The Servant is Stricken Internally!'

Four things seem to stand out in this strophe or stanza and we want to watch for them: **First**, the intensity of the suffering; note the words in these verses, grief, sorrow, stricken, smitten, afflicted, wounded, bruised or crushed, chastisement, stripes, laid upon; all are descriptive of suffering and physical violence. **Second**, the vicarious suffering, not merely suffering with men but for men, our griefs, our sorrows, our transgressions, our iniquities, our peace was laid upon Him. **Third**, the moral necessity of the suffering; mankind was estranged from God, "all we like sheep have gone astray (*ta-ah #8582* – to mislead or deceive ourselves)…" and the LORD laid on Him the iniquity of the world! I can't fathom that, can you? The iniquity of the world! I John 2:2 says, "He is the propitiation for the whole (holos) world (kosmos)." **Fourth**, the peace that comes from suffering, "the chastisement for our peace was upon Him." The word peace is a sweet, strong, suggestive word and means wholeness or 'at-one-ness' and therefore refers to a rich, harmonious relationship. When you are at peace you are in harmony!

It's one thing to suffer and die, it's quite another thing to suffer **infinitely** and not be able to die! Now I can't quite fathom that, can you? I personally have been very close to death on several occasions, but I have never been close to death and couldn't die, have you?

In v.3 the Servant our Messiah became intimate (*yada*) (familiar, acquainted, affectionate) with our grief. We endure pain, grief, sorrow and suffering but He became intimate with it and for our sakes, **"He embraced it!"** He hugged it! Can you understand that? He became intimate with our grief, sorrow, pain, suffering, sin, intimate! Will we ever really understand what intimacy with sin really meant on Calvary? What it really meant to become, "acquainted with grief?" I don't think so! Will we ever know the depth and the magnitude of His suffering, I hardly doubt it? Can we share in His suffering, His shame, and His solitude? I believe we can, to a degree, anyway....

In the Newer Testament, Paul said in Phil. 3:10, "That I may know Him (*ginosko* - to know by experience) the **power** of His resurrection, and the **fellowship** of His sufferings, being made **conformable** unto His death;" (Can you pray that? Do you pray that?) Do you really want to be more like Jesus? Be honest? Peter did, I Pet. 4:13 says, "But rejoice inasmuch as ye are partakers of Christ's __suffering's__ that when His glory shall be revealed, ye may be glad also with __exceeding joy__." (Not just joy – but (*agalliao*) exceeding joy! Over abundant joy!)

However, I believe Romans 8:18 is the key verse on this when Paul said, "For I reckon that the __sufferings__ of this present time are not __worthy__ to be compared with the __glory__ which shall be revealed in us." **"WOW!"** (Having a rough day? Read 2 Cor. 11:23-33) Compared to Christ on the cross your problem isn't a problem at all! Not if you can still scratch your nose!

I don't think we can suffer the '__Infinite wrath of God__' because we are __finite beings__, but we can suffer __finitely__ for a long time! For the ultimate glory of God! Amen? You see it is God's will for every one of us to be "__Saved__, __Sealed__, __Sanctified__, __Spirit Filled__, __Serving__ and to __Suffer,__ " some a little, some a lot. That's His will for every child of His! Read Romans 5:1-11, aloud to someone!

I don't know how suffering works in God's economy of things, but I do know this, 'God is glorified in our __suffering__!' Glorified my friend, __GLORIFIED__! He was glorified in His Son's suffering and He is glorified in yours and mine! If God has called you to suffer then do it and do it quietly!

"Surely He has borne our griefs...," Surely (*aw-kane*) truly, indeed, verily, certainly, nevertheless, 'assuredly;' This word has a strong, assertive force. Like 'Verily, Verily; Truly, Truly; Amen, Amen.' This word is emphasizing a contrast to v.3, but on the contrary; but in fact; but yet; It is linked with another very strong word 'borne' (*nasa*) to lift, bear up, carry off, take away, to be swept away, to bear continuously. Not just removing but lifting it up and carrying it away. This Servant did not become a sinner, He bore our sins away, which is very important!

This word is used of an 'Armor Bearer' eighteen times in the Older Testament and in Leviticus with sacrifices for propitiation and expiation. (*ek-spe-a-tion*). Two very, very strong words to emphasize the very great burden He had to bear namely, yours and mine! (All the pronouns in these verses are "emphatic" for emphasis!)

This word borne (*nasa*) also shows us He is not merely entering into our miseries and pain but it portrays a complete gathering together unto Himself of all the legal, judicial sentences of sufferings which we deserved to endure. This verse encompasses the true tone of substitutionary atonement in total, II Cor. 5:21; and it answers the age old question of Matt. 27:46, "*Eli, Eli, lama sabachthani*, 'My God, My God, why have You forsaken Me?" Because legally God had to turn His back on His Son, the Messiah, because He had the legal, judicial sentence of the (*kosmos*) the world, upon Himself at the cross!

Because the word (*nasa*) to bear up or away, is used in connection with the sacrifices of expiation in Lev. 5:1, 17; 16:22; 20:19, 20; His suffering was expiatory (*ek-spe-a-tor-e* – what a powerful word in meaning and doctrine, just difficult to pronounce) meaning, to put an end to, to extinguish the guilt incurred and it is vicarious in nature. He also bore our 'Griefs' (*kholee*) afflictions, sickness, anxiety, and injuries. It does not refer to sin but to suffering, and it's from a primitive root to become weak, sick, diseased, grieved, sorrow; literally, "spiritual sickness."

This word is also used in a metaphorical sense for pain, sorrow and evil, i.e., human ills and trials in life. (lit; to take the burden from one's shoulders and put it on His own and carry it away!) He will expiate, extinguish all your pain and sorrow if you will let Him, that's also why He went to the Cross at Calvary. Think of the cross, if you will, as a sin/fire extinguisher!" He will extinguish the guilt and pain. "He has borne (*nasa*) all our griefs, all our afflictions, all our anxieties (*kholee*)..." (To the bitter end – (*te-tel-es-tai*) 'It is Finished!') **"IF"** we will just give them to Him!! That is the key! **IF?** The big two letter word!

"And carried our sorrows..." The word 'Carried' (*sabal*) means to labor under a load or burden, to drag along, to be heavy laden; It's found 23x in the O. T. and it's used of a burden so heavy it has to be dragged along. What is it that is so heavy that it has to be dragged along? <u>Our 'Sorrows'</u> (*mak-ob*) <u>our</u> pain and sorrow both physical and mental or spiritual. The key here is that they acknowledge that this Servant did not suffer for His own sins but that He carried upon His shoulders the burden of their sins and the pain of their transgressions. His suffering was expiatory and vicarious in nature.

Sorrow (*mak-ob*) refers more to mental pain, whereas, grief (*kho-lee*) refers more to physical pain. Sometimes 'Mental Pain' is much more severe than physical pain, you can't take two aspirins and lie down and make it go away in two hours! Amen? Sometimes it never goes away, is that where that phrase, "Time heals all wounds" comes in? Physical pain does not make you sweat great drops of blood (*hematohidrosis*) but mental pain and anguish can. Luke 22:44. This word is also translated 'Marred.' Similar to Isa. 52:14 but there a different word is used to show total disfigurement of His face. (*mo-shat*) (His visage (face) was soooo marred...)

Here it's His Spirit that is disfigured; it's the inner pain and anguish, "My God, My God, why have You forsaken Me?" *(Eli, Eli, lama sabachthani?)* <u>His Spirit is disfigured</u>!! (distraught, twisted, deformed, distorted). He bore our burdens and griefs like an 'Armor Bearer' and He carried or dragged along our sorrows, our physical and mental sufferings like a work animal drags a heavy load along the road, one tough step at a time! And what do we do? We esteem Him! We value Him!

But Wait! Who is the **'WE'** in v.4? In v.3, the **'WE'** hid their faces from Him and wouldn't esteem Him or value Him! But now as a 'Burden-Bearer' and 'Sorrow-Carrier' the **WE**, in v. 4, 'Esteem Him; Reckon Him; Value Him; Regard Him – <u>But How</u>?

"Yet WE did esteem Him <u>stricken</u>, <u>smitten</u> of God, and <u>afflicted</u>!!" If Israel is the Servant, then who is the **'We'** in this verse? **We** did esteem (*khsab*) consider, account, regard, reckon, impute, Him; This Servant 'Stricken' (*naga*) in the sense of being blasted, cast down, down trodden, plagued, to strike violently.

In Exodus 12:22 they took a bunch of hyssop, three sprigs and bound them together in an (*echad*) plunged it into the blood of the lamb in the basin at the front door and (*naga*) struck the lentil of the door. Then they dipped the bunch of hyssop in the basin of blood a second time and with one stroke (*naga*) struck the two door posts or (*mezuzot*) leaving a sign, a mark, an (*owth*) on the door for the destroyer to see that night, the (*Masheit*) the death angel in Exodus 12:23.

Not only was this Servant/Messiah 'Stricken' (*naga*) Isaiah says He was also 'Smitten' (*naka*) to slay, to beat, to kill, to slaughter or scourge! This is Divine retribution for a heinous crime or sin! This is a very, very strong word and means to be fatally smitten, killed or slain! To be attacked, ravaged, destroyed! Are you getting the picture? Not very pleasant is it? It takes you back to Isaiah 52:14-15 where, "His visage was sooo marred more than any man and His form more than the sons of men." Marred – (*moshat*) deformed, disfigured, corrupted, implying ugly and repulsive!

This Servant/Messiah was not just 'Smitten' (*naga*) but 'Stricken' (*naka*) as well. In the sense of being blasted like King *Uzziah,* who was stricken with leprosy when he stepped into the priesthood for a moment. (It was just for a moment – it was just incense – it was just leprosy!)

Smitten, means to be inflicted with a curse! What curse? Gen. 3, the 'Sin and the thorns.' The thorns were the result of the sin in the garden. This Servant not only bore our sin, and dragged our griefs along, but he wore our 2" thorns on His head and they were beaten down through His skull with His staff.

Listen, death and sin are universal, "It is appointed unto men once to die, but after this the judgement, (the condemnation, damnation, punishment)." Heb. 9:27. Judgement (*kri-sis*) what English word do you think we get from this Greek word? (Crisis – The turning point! Like mid-life crisis!)

Second, you are not a sinner because you sin, you sin because you are a sinner, it's in your nature. As a bird is born to fly, and a fish is born to swim, man is born to sin! You don't have to teach a two year old to lie, to steal, to rebel, to hit, to loose its temper, to throw things, to bite people, you have to teach them 'NOT' to do those things! Romans 5:12 says, "Wherefore, as by one man (*Adam*) sin entered into the world and death by sin, and so death passed upon **ALL** men, for **ALL** have sinned."

Stricken by Whom v.4? By God, (*Elohim*) The God of creation! Only God has the Right, the Power, the Authority, the Majesty, to strike the Servant, the Messiah, His Son, Ps. 2:7; Prov. 30:4; Acts 13:33; Heb. 1:5; Heb. 5:5. This false doctrine called **'Deicide'** is nonsense. How could a man with an ounce of intelligence ever conceive of another man killing God? That's ludicrous, ridiculous, absurd, preposterous, bizarre, laughable and would even be comical if it wasn't so stupid!

Let me clear something up; The Jewish people did not kill the Messiah *Yeshua*/Jesus, they couldn't! The Romans did not kill the Jewish Messiah *Yeshua*/Jesus, they couldn't! It was our sin that put Him on that tree and made Him sweat, 'great drops of blood,' and cry giant, strong, powerful, forceful (*ischyros*) tears. Heb. 5:7. But it was God, *Elohim* Who smote Him and struck Him (*naga - naka*) and cursed Him with a curse, Gal. 3:13, because of our stinking sin. Not that He was actually stricken by God, but we (you and I) esteemed Him, accounted Him to be so! He bore our sin, in His body, on our tree, on Calvary 2,000 years ago!

It is based on this verse that the Talmud refers to the Messiah as, 'The Leprous One.' The Babylonian Talmud, Sanhedrin 98b says of Isaiah 53:4, "The Messiah, what is his name?" The Rabbis say, 'the leprous one' those of the house of Rabbi say, 'the sick one' as it is said, "surely he hath borne our sickness." Why, "The Leprous One!" Because (*naga*) is used of striking a person with leprosy, like King *Uzziah* in II Chron. 26:20.

He is shunned like a leper when he carries, or drags along our griefs, our sorrows, and our sins. What does a leper cry out? **Unclean! Unclean! Unclean!** And everyone turns away, no one wants to look at a leper, no one! It was because of all this that He cried from the tree, *"Eli. Eli, Lama Sabachthani..."* Psalm 22:1.

The answer as we have said is in Psalm 22:3, because God is holy; Isa. 6:3; and God had to turn away, why? Hab. 1:13, God can't look on iniquity, because of His holiness! But we never turn away, we never turn our backs on 'The Savior,' we are never ashamed of the Messiah of Israel, are we Peter???

"*Naga - Naka*," Stricken and Smitten of God, but it doesn't end there, Oh I wish it did, but there is one more! Stricken, Smitten and 'Afflicted' (*anah*) humbled, humiliated; to bow down, to stoop down, to mistreat, to dishonor, or to ravish! **"Stricken, Smitten, Afflicted,"** three words to describe His Hell on earth! I don't fully understand this, and I am not going to try to explain it, I just accept it, embrace it, praise Him for it and go on!

Stricken of God (*naga*) refers to a loathsome disease like leprosy; Smitten of God (*naka*) refers to divine retribution for heinous sin; Afflicted of God (*anah*) refers to punishment for one's crime. All describing the terrible, horrible consequences and penalty of our sin.

Maimonides in the 12th century said, "*Yeshua*/Jesus deserved the violent death He suffered." Deserved It! Nobody deserved this, Nobody! Most of all, not the, 'Man from Nazareth!' "Who had done no violence, neither was any deceit found in His mouth." Isa. 53:9.

The fact that the Leaders of *Yeshua*/Jesus' day attempted to prove He was a blasphemer and not equal to God the Father, and did miracles on the Sabbath Day, and healed the blind, the lame, the deaf, the lepers, and raised the dead, and cast out demons that only the Devil could do; Showed He deserved to die, fulfilling this prophecy in amazing detail. "He (Christ) was despised and we (Leaders) esteemed Him not!"

"Surely He has borne **OUR** griefs, and carried **OUR** sorrows, yet **WE** did esteem Him stricken, smitten of God and afflicted." Isaiah 53:4. How prophetic is that? Or should I say, "How pathetic is that?" This verse reminds me of an old hymn lost to our churches and young people today, "Amazing Love, how can it be, that Thou my God, should die for me."

Mashiach bore our sins as though they were His own, He bore the pain, the punishment and made atonement for the whole world. He took the blame and then vicariously suffered the shame, as though He was the guilty one. Yet we esteemed Him stricken, inflicted with a curse; judicially afflicted as a leper; and smitten by God as a rebel, defeated, crushed and condemned!

All this led Him to Calvary, but does it lead you to Calvary? The Cross is not just something we come to for Salvation; it's something we cling to for assurance, service, hope, comfort, strength, direction, guidance, etc. But it's also a special reminder of just how much He really loves us! Do you know Him? Do you really, really know (*yada*) Him? In your **heart**, not your **head**! Hos. 6:3! He is not talking about knowing about the LORD, he's talking about a personal relationship with *YeHoVaH*, the *YHVH*, the *GOD* of redemption and His Son, Jesus The Christ? (Ps. 46:10)

PRAYER - "Father, I have no words to utter as I sit here, my heart is silent, my spirit is full, my soul is overwhelmed. I cannot even begin to fathom what Your Servant, Your Messiah, Your only begotten Son went through for **US**. I can't thank You enough for Your sacrifice but I hope You know **WE** appreciate everything You did for **US**. We come to You now and bare our hearts and souls before You and beg Your forgiveness. In Jesus' name, Amen!"

****

Part Two: The Servant Wounded Fatally – Isa. 53:5

As I finished writing Isa. 53:4, "The Servant Afflicted Mercilessly," I sat at my desk in tears, overwhelmed by emotion because of what God's Servant had to go through for me. He bore 'our' grief's, he dragged 'our' sorrows along like a burdened animal, and we esteemed him stricken, smitten and afflicted (*naga, naka, anah*) and this was done by God, but why?

Isaiah 53:5 gives us the answer to that question, although we may not like the answer. "But He was wounded for our transgressions; He was bruised for our iniquities; The chastisement for our peace was upon Him; And with His stripes we are healed." KJV 1967. Or, "But he was wounded because of our transgressions, he was crushed because of our iniquities; The chastisement of our welfare was upon him, And with his stripes we were healed." JPS, 1966.

In v.4 we have the 'Ministry of the Servant,' but in v. 5 we have the 'Sufferings of the Servant.' What is amazing is that in vv. 5-6 we have six references to sin and in each occasion a different word is used to describe it: <u>Transgression</u>: (*pasha*) rebellion, revolt, the crossing of a boundary and trespassing on a foreign land; <u>Iniquities</u>: (*avon*) wickedness, the absence of equity or the absence of dealing justly, with a focus on the guilt and liability incurred; <u>Discord</u>: the opposite of peace, which is enmity between us and God; <u>Disease</u> of the spirit: which is impossible to heal; <u>Willful wandering</u>: like that of a wayward sheep; A '<u>Heavy Burden</u>:' so immense it was literally smashing or crushing Him into the earth.

Note also the 'four' pronoun comparisons in v. 5 between 'he and our.' If the Servant is the nation of Israel, then who is the 'our and we' in v. 5? The comparison is noted by Isaiah, not once but four times!

"But '<u>He</u>' was wounded for '<u>our</u>' transgressions;" The words 'But He' in this verse are an emphatic assertion, that the real cause of his suffering, was not for his own sins but for the transgressions of his people as pointed out by the pronoun 'our.' The word 'wounded' (*meholal*) means to pierce through, to bore through, to perforate; hence, to wound, or to be tormented, or to writhe in pain. It was a common belief that the Messiah would be violently put to death!

We can never hope to understand nor comprehend the 'Atonement.' It's an infinite truth and we are finite beings. There was a God-ward as well as a Man-ward aspect to it, but into the "Cup" His Father gave Him to drink no man, no angel, in fact no created being of any sort has the power or right to look, not even a glimpse!

It is not enough to say that the pride of the Jewish people, or the scorn of the Greeks, or the power of the Romans crucified Jesus Christ! He was, "Delivered up by God for our offences!" There is no stronger word in the Hebrew language to portray a violent and painful death, none! The word writhe or tormented is added in some Bible margins due to the Hebrew meaning of pierced!

His hands, his feet, his side, even his head were all pierced, perforated and bored through!! It is amazing that the word 'pierced' was used here of the Servant, Messiah's death instead of hanged, stoned, or beheaded which were the only Jewish methods of execution used in Isaiah's time. Crucifixion as a means of execution was invented by the Carthaginians and perfected by the Romans, 700 years after Isaiah's time. Here is a strong testimony to the inspiration of the prophetic Scriptures.

You will also find the word 'pierced' in Ps. 22:16 and Zech. 12:10 but there you will find two different Hebrew words used; Ps. 22 uses (*kara*); Zech. 12 uses (*daqar*); Isa. 53 uses (*halel*). This one is speaking of being mortally and brutally wounded, literally pierced, or bored through to the point of death, for our transgressions, our rebellions, our lawlessness! He was pierced, bored, transfixed, hence nailed *for* or (on account of) our (*pesha*) transgressions, rebellions against human and divine authority. I am having trouble comprehending this, are you?

Nailed for our (*pesha*) transgressions which were really rebellions. The pain was really His, in consequence for the sin which was really ours, yours and mine and we deserved the pain too! Rebellion is the primary element in all human sin. Transgressions can come in many forms like missing the mark through aimlessness, carelessness or a wrong aim. Or coming up short even though your work may be alright in its direction but it just doesn't come up to God's standard. Which is absolute perfection in thought, word and deed! Then you can transgress by crossing a boundary and going over to the wrong side altogether. WOW!! So much to comprehend; So much to take in!!

Then, "He' was bruised for 'our' iniquities;" The word bruised (*daka*) means to break into little pieces, to crush, or shatter, 'into a million pieces,' to use a colloquial expression. This word designates the most severe inward and outward sufferings imaginable; this same word is used for pounding into dust, to pulverize! He was rendered listless, lethargic and languid. He was under such a weight of sorrows on account of our sins, that he was, as it were, crushed to the earth. (Let's pause! Catch our breath! Go get a cup of tea! Take an Intermission!)

At this point Psalm 85:10-11 was brought to its fullest development, *"Mercy and truth, are met together; righteousness and peace, have kissed each other. Truth shall spring out of the earth, and righteousness shall look down from heaven."* **WOW!! What a beautiful Psalm!** Psalm 110:7 says, "He shall drink of the brook/valley (*nahal- wadi*) in the way/wayside (*derek*

– road, path, trail) therefore shall He lift up the head." This Servant journeyed to our earth and humbled himself by drinking out of our 'mud-puddle.' How is that for humility?

On the cross Christ was "Bruised" which means, 'crushed under the weight of a burden!' What burden? Our sin! Ps. 38:4, "For my iniquities are gone over my head; like a heavy burden, they are too heavy for me." Imagine the burden of the sin of the whole (*kosmos*) or world! Can you even fathom that? For 'our' iniquities, not His, our (*avon*) our sin, our wickedness, our iniquity; often with a focus on the guilt or liability incurred, and the punishment to follow.

This statement indicates that the Servant, the Messiah was shattered, crushed for our 'inborn crookedness.' The words "bruised & crushed" are among the strongest in the Hebrew language and denote a violent, fierce, extreme, vicious, painful death! The root signifies to 'bend or twist' and refers to the tortuous, crooked winding ways of men when they conform to no standard at all, except their own, and walk according to the wicked course of this world, and it is wicked.

The Hebrew word (*medhukkah*) means utterly crushed and shattered and (*avonoth*) means not only 'iniquities' but 'twisted and perverted crookedness.' In other words our sin principle is basically an incorrigible perversity and He bore it all, every bit of it! Sin is very serious, Isaiah calls it 'Transgression' rebellion against God, daring to cross the line God has drawn, vv. 5 & 8. He also calls it 'Iniquity' crookedness of our sinful nature, vv. 5 & 6. Therefore, we are sinners by choice and sinners by nature; wicked, perverse, incorrigible, twisted, hell-bent sinners!

"The chastisement of 'our' peace was upon 'Him;'" The word chastisement (*musar*) means correction, chastening, punishment, disciplinary sufferings; for our peace (*shlo-*menu) peace, safety, prosperity, welfare was upon Him; 'the chastisement which secured our peace.' Peace usually has the idea of well-being, but here it is much more! For forgiveness to be real it must be secured at a price, a very high price! He was chastised and given many stripes, too many to count and yet that chastisement brought us peace!

In order to forgive sinners, a righteous God must base His forgiveness on moral grounds. Otherwise His forgiveness would be morally unacceptable and spiritually meaningless. The only way a law-breaker can be at peace with the law is to suffer the punishment that the law demands. (Pay the fine and do the time!)

Why? Because there would be no difference between righteousness and wickedness? However, the Creator of all mankind, Elohim is not only merciful but He is also righteous and just! Rom. 3:26 says, "That He might be just and the justifier of him who believes in Jesus."

So, the righteous Servant, the Messiah of God took upon Himself the chastisement which secured our (***Shalom***)! Isaiah 26:3 says, "Thou wilt keep him in perfect peace, (*shalom, shalom*) whose mind is stayed upon Thee, because he trusts in Thee." Therefore, Jesus kept the law perfectly, yet He suffered the punishment that belonged to us and because He took our place we now have peace with God and cannot be condemned by God's law. Rom. 5:1 says, "Therefore being justified by faith, we have peace with God through our Lord Jesus Christ." Rom. 8:1.

Perfect peace, is peace on the outside and peace on the inside. The only way there will be true, "Peace on earth" is when the Servant/Messiah sets up His throne in Jerusalem and reigns over the whole earth. Likewise, the only way there will be true peace in my heart and in your heart and life is for you and me to surrender our lives to Him and give up the throne room of our hearts and let Him reign there right now. Peace stands for the individual designation of our salvation! You must give up the 'Right to Yourself' to Jesus Christ! All of it! You must let this Servant of YeHoVaH, Jesus the Christ, have the key to the throne room of your heart!

At Passover Jewish people quote, Psalm 116:12-13, "What shall I render unto the LORD for all of His benefits toward me? (I know) I will take the cup of salvation (the cup of *Yeshua*) and call on the name of the LORD." That's 'Perfect Peace!' Something all Israel and all the Jewish people long for and pray for every day, PEACE! Perfect peace, *Shalom, Shalom*; Peace on the outside and peace on the inside.

"Having abolished in His flesh the enmity, even the law of commandments contained in ordinances, to make in Himself of the two one new man, so making peace;" Eph. 2:15. We can now maintain a peaceful disposition toward God, not only having **peace with God,** Rom. 5:1, but the **peace of God**, Phil. 4:6-7, and there is a big difference. Amen? Once you have made peace with God and you have the peace of God, you will receive peace from God. Col. 1:2; Rom. 1:7; I Cor. 1:3; II Cor. 1:2; Gal. 1:3; Eph. 1:2; Phil. 1:2; etc.

The punishment, the chastisement, that secured our peace, was laid upon Him, and He bore it for us and all we have to do is reach out and receive it, because it's a free gift. Free to us, but it was not 'Free' to God, it cost Him immensely; His only unique Son, Jesus The Christ!

"And with 'His' stripes 'we' are (were) healed." Literally, 'it has been healed for us.' Healing in this context is primarily the healing of the soul from the sickness of sin. Yet in addition to the spiritual healing, physical and emotional healing may be included as well. It is a known fact that physical ailments tend to have an emotional, psychic background, but the context is sin.

The word stripes (*habbura*) means blows, wounds, bruises, welts and blueness. Some people translate this, black and blue marks, a flesh wound that does not draw blood and some translate it just bruising, obviously they have never read nor studied the whole passage. The Hebrew word 'stripes is singular' but it is used with the force of a **collective** so that it may be translated "stripes or wounds."

Others translate this word, 'Blows that cut to the very bone; Blows that leave a visible imprint; Deep life threatening blows.' Maybe from a whip or a 'Cat-of-nine-tails,' with pieces of metal or bone attached to the ends to rip pieces of flesh out with each blow inflicted! We are healed, or literally, 'it is healed to us,' or 'healing has happened to us.'

The question to ask or pose; Is the context talking about sin or sickness? In Matthew chapter eight in the Newer Testament the Messiah healed the leper, the centurion's servant, Peter's mother-in-law, and all who were sick or demon possessed; ALL! The Greek tense there is time present which is very important! You can't carry it forward 2,000 years! He stilled the storm and cast out demons, to give evidence of His Messiahship and Deity and everyone who came for healing was healed, everyone!

So, Matthew quotes Isaiah 53:5 in Peter's house (Matt. 8:17) In fact Peter later made it very clear in I Peter 2:24-25 that the Servant or Messiah's wounds heal us from sin, not from disease! After all, it was Peter's mother-in-law in Matt. 8:16-17 who was healed. The Servant didn't go to Calvary because we were sick; <u>He died on the cross because we are sinners</u>! The healing referred to here is spiritual healing, or healing from sin. Pardon from sin, and restoration to favor with God, are not infrequently represented as an act of healing in the Scriptures.

The figure is derived from the fact that awakened and convicted sinners are often represented as crushed, broken, and bruised by the weight of their transgressions, and the removal of the load of sin is represented as an act of healing. Ps. 41:4 says, "I said, LORD, be merciful unto me, heal my soul; for I have sinned against Thee." Psalm 51 will tear your heart out by the roots. Listen to v.17, "The sacrifices of God are a broken spirit; a broken and a contrite heart, O God, thou wilt not despise." (Are those your sacrifices today?) Ps. 6:2 says, "Have mercy upon me O LORD; for I am weak. O LORD, heal me; for my bones are vexed." Ps. 103:3 says, "Who forgives all thine iniquities, who heals all thy diseases."

The idea here is that the Servant or Messiah would be scourged and that it would be by that scourging that health or healing would be imparted to our souls. Healing in the atonement was fulfilled during Christ's life not after His death.

One author put it this way: "Disease and death cannot be permanently removed until sin is permanently removed and *the Messiah's* supreme work was to conquer sin." In the atonement He dealt with sin, death & sickness; and yet all three of those are still with us. When He died on the tree, He bruised the head of Satan and broke the <u>power of sin</u> and the person who trusts in His atoning work is immediately delivered from the <u>penalty of sin</u> and one day will be delivered from the very <u>presence of sin</u> and its consequences, and its power, one day but not yet!

The ultimate fulfillment of His redeeming work is yet future for believers (Rom. 8:22-25; 13:11). The Servant/Messiah died for man's sin, but His followers still die or should I say sin; He overcame pain and sickness but His followers still suffer and become ill. There is physical healing in the atonement, just as there is total deliverance from sin and death in the atonement; but we still await the fulfillment of that deliverance in the day when the LORD brings an end to suffering, sin and death.

Those who claim that His followers should never be sick because there is healing in the atonement should also claim that His followers should never die, because He also conquered death in the atonement. The central passage of the gospel is deliverance from sin. It is the good news about forgiveness, not health. The Messiah was made sin, not disease and He died on the tree for our sin, not our sickness. Paul wrote in I Cor. 15:3, "For I delivered unto you first of all that which I also received, that <u>Christ died for our sins</u> according to the Scriptures;" (Not our Sickness!)

The Servant's sufferings are not only vicarious but redemptive and curative. The doctrine of divine healing has too often been neglected and left for the perversion of fanatics, but it must be addressed in its context with civility and decorum. "LORD, what is there for us to say; pierced, crushed, chastised, striped, cut to the bone, for what?" For our transgressions, for our iniquities, for our peace, for our sin, for our soul, for Your glory!

"But **He** was pierced through for **our** transgressions; **He** was crushed for **our** iniquities; The chastening for **our** well-being fell upon **Him**; And by **His** scourging **we** are healed." NASB When a man is healed by the stripes of another, his only instinct and response should be, "I will spend the rest of my life and all the strength I have, as a healed man, for Him who healed me!" "Thank You Lord, now use us, spread us, sow us, for Your glory, in Your name we pray." Amen!

Father, there are no words to express what is on our hearts, we have no right to drink from the cup Your Son drank from or even to look on its contents, or to be baptized with the baptism He was baptized with, or to walk where He walked. But we are Your children, joint heirs with Christ and he has given us access into Your presence and we cry out with the Seraphim, 'Holy, Holy, Holy' is the LORD God Almighty. Father, hear our prayer!

Part Three: The Servant Stricken Internally – Isa. 53:6

Isaiah 53:6 has often been referred to as, "The John 3:16 of the Older Testament." Why? Because it too, is the Gospel, or the 'Good News' in a nutshell! **First**, it shows the analysis of sin and its effects, "All...have willfully gone astray;" **Second**, it shows a description of Mt. Calvary's or Mt. Moriah's execution, "The LORD (*YHVH*) has laid (*paga*) upon Him, His Servant, His Messiah our penalty;" **Third**, it shows the scope of the atonement, "The iniquity (*avon*) of us All."

This verse begins with the word 'ALL' and ends with the word 'ALL' (*kol*) any, every, the whole, the totality of the masses, the (*kosmos*) the whole world! Every person who ever lived or who will ever live! I Jn. 2:2 says, "And He is the propitiation (the satisfying sacrifice) for our sins, and not for ours only…but for the whole world!"

This was one of D. L. Moody's favorite verses, and when he was boarding a train, a young man, probably Jewish, ran up and asked him how he might receive eternal life? Moody told him to go home and read Isaiah 53:6, to which he responded, "But what do I do with it?" and Moody said: "Go in on the first 'ALL' and out on the last 'ALL'!" The young man went home, opened his Bible, read the verse several times, fell on his knees and received God's free gift of eternal life. No wonder Wesley wrote, "Amazing love how can it be, that Thou my God should'st die for me."

Now to look at the Bible in miniature, Isaiah 53:6, **"All we like sheep, have gone astray;"** How many? Most, many, multitudes? No, "All we," (*kallanu*) it is an emphatic assertion concerning all people, any, every, the whole! The totality of the masses, without one exception! The (*kosmos*) the whole (*holos*) I John 2:2 world and all its inhabitants!

"Have gone astray!" That means every human being alive has an innate bent to stray or wander from the paths of righteousness and we do it intentionally. It's in our very nature, too wander! Sheep (*ts-one*) is from an unused root to migrate, in fact straying is characteristic of sheep, they are totally dependent on a shepherd, leader or protector, **totally dependent**! You lead sheep or a flock with a staff, walking before them, but you drive cattle or a herd with a whip, riding behind them! Sheep don't fear danger, they walk right into it head first. That's why sheep need direction and a director or shepherd/pastor to lead them. Sheep without a shepherd are lost and totally defenseless and will die in the wilderness. In Matt. 9:36 *Yeshua/Jesus* looked upon Israel as, "sheep having no shepherd."

However, as I said sheep have a tendency to, **"go astray,"** to err, to wander and are easily led astray (*ta'ah*) wander off course so as to get into trouble, in fact it's in their very nature to do so. Sheep also go astray ungratefully, they forsake the hand that feeds them and heals their diseases, picks the bugs off and even bite it on occasion and they go astray repeatedly. If restored today, they will go astray tomorrow if not today and wander even further and further, from bad to worse. There's no limit to their wandering except their own frailty, and when they get tired they just lay down.

This is Isaiah's vivid description of how humanity behaves, as well as God's analogy of Adam's descendants. This clause is also the confession of a repentant Israel: In the Alpha Psalm, the last verse 119:176 says, "I have gone astray like a lost sheep." It also portrays a repentant humanity in I Pet. 2:25 which says, "For ye were as sheep going astray, but are now returned unto the Shepherd and Bishop of your souls." What a great analogy of mankind, God could not have compared us with a better animal. "All we like sheep have gone astray," (past tense) "and!"

"We have turned every one to his own way," Nothing could more strikingly represent the condition of mankind then this phrase. We have turned from God, and are following our own paths, we are pursuing our own pleasures, and we are exposed to every kind of danger known to man, beast or demon! We have turned (*pan-ah*) turned away, turned back from following the Chief Shepherd, 'The Bishop of our souls." Every one (*eesh*) every man, person, being, has turned to "his own way." His own road, journey, path, direction, course of life or moral character. Read - (Rom. 6:21-23).

Man prefers his own way to God's way. He has transferred his allegiance to the idol of his heart, namely himself; His will, his desires, his intellect and innate tendencies to be wholly selfish. That is man's common guilt, and goal; Gen. 3:5, "Ye shall be as gods." We need to give up the throne of our hearts to this Servant, the Messiah and the sooner the better.

In other words, we need to get out of the Savior business! Proverbs 14:12 says, "There is a *way* (singular) which seems right unto a man, but the end thereof are the *ways* (plural) of death." There are many ways to the Messiah, the highway, the roadway, the pathway, the byway, the throughway (we all came a different way to Jesus); But there is only one way to God the Father and that is through Israel's Messiah! John 14:6 in the Newer Testament tells us what that way is for the Jew and the Gentile! And that leads us to the third phrase:

"And the LORD has laid on Him," The (*YHVH*) Jehovah, The I AM, The Self-Existent One! (*Ehyeh, Asher, Ehyeh*). When you see the name Jehovah - **LORD**, you are dealing with redemption and the covenant keeping God. When you see the name Elohim - **God**, you are dealing with creation and the Creator of all mankind.

In v. 4, the Servant was stricken and smitten (*naga - naka*) violently, like a leper by Elohim – God, the One Who created all things. However, in v. 6 it is the LORD - Jehovah, the God of Redemption, **Who laid (*pa-ga* – our iniquities) on Him**; to strike violently, to fall upon; in a hostile sense, to attack with the idea of violence leading to death; to kill, to slay, to impinge, (two objects coming together with such force they are totally inseparable).

This same verb is used in I Kings 2:34, "So *Benaiah* fell upon him and slew him." All gentleness is completely excluded from this verse on purpose. No stronger language can be used to explain expiation for sin, for all mankind. NONE! What martyr, what group of people would you place here as the ultimate, infinite sacrifice for all mankind? Can you think of any? I can't think of one either!

The word (*paga*) can also be translated **'meet;'** "The LORD has made to 'meet' on Him the iniquity of us all." (I put this in, in case you have one of those sissy translations in your hands: "Like a boxer's right hook that meets his opponents left jaw…" Problem: It does not have the same force as *'laid upon Him'* but it still can paint a nice picture of atonement. The meeting place of sin is the mercy-seat (*kapporet*) of sinners; a bloody, messy, smelly place! By the way, whose job was it to clean it up every day anyway?

However: The end result is the same either way; If you will not consent that your iniquities shall meet upon Israel's Messiah, then you must bear them yourself, alone! (Scary thought, Amen?) Again Ps. 85:10 culminates right here, "Mercy and truth are **met** together; righteousness and peace have **kissed** each other." I love that word picture, don't you? That leads us to the last phrase:

"The iniquity of us all." The LORD has laid (*paga*) on Him, His Servant, the Messiah, His Son, 'the iniquity (*avon*) depravity, perversity, lawlessness, of us all!' You wonder sometimes, don't you, just how bad man's heart really is; How wicked is wicked, how depraved is depraved and then you study Isaiah 53:5 and you see that the Messiah was crushed, shattered to dust, (the same word) rendered listless, lethargic, and languid and literally crushed to the earth by our 'inborn crookedness.' WOW!

The root of (*avon*) means 'twisted, perverted, crookedness.' In other words our sin nature is basically an incorrigible perversity and He nailed it to the tree for you and for me. Col. 2:14 ® "He nailed it to the tree!" There is no stronger language in Hebrew to denote the fact that, His sufferings were to make atonement (*katallagay* – mutual exchange) for all (*kol*) mankind. **NONE!** Jehovah, violently loaded on Him our distorted, twisted, perverted sin nature.

Our sin is no different to God than the sin you find on the street, in the slums, the gutters, the allies, or skid row. Don't sugar coat yours, to God sin is sin and it cost Him His Son! Gen. 6:5 says we are all sinners by nature, **"Every** imagination of man's heart is only evil continually!" (Every imagination of your heart & mine is only evil continually).

Do you really want to know what God thinks about your good deeds, your righteousness, and your (*mitzvoth)*? Here is Isaiah 64:6 from the Roman Catholic Bible, "And we are all become as one unclean, and all our justices as the rag of a menstruous woman: and we have all fallen as a leaf, and our iniquities like the wind, have taken us away." That's what God thinks about your good deeds, imagine what He thinks about your bad ones!

Ecc. 7:20 tells us we are all sinners by practice, "For there is not a just man upon earth, that does good and sins not." (Rom. 3:10-12) 'No Not One!' As a fish is born to swim and a bird is born to fly, man is born to sin, it's in our nature. We are not sinners because we sin; we sin because we were born sinners.

This Servant became our Sin-Bearer to remove the Sin-Barrier, which was preventing us from entering into God's presence. Listen, He was forsaken so we never would have to be. That is substitutionary, vicarious atonement! God became man and died on a tree for you and for me! Not because it was fun but because it had to be done! He bought your chocolates! Happy Valentines Day!

The cauldron of Almighty God's infinite wrath was poured out upon His Servant, the Messiah. A finite creature could not have borne God's infinite wrath, so the Suffering Servant had to be the Messiah who provided the vicarious atonement and bore the iniquities of the world, the (*kosmos*).

What does it mean to suffer the infinite wrath of God? I don't know, and I don't ever want to know, but I do know this, He did it for you and for me because He loves us, that much I know. It was love that held Him on that tree on Calvary not the nails, LOVE! Agape love, sacrificial love, love that gives, and gives, and gives and asks nothing in return, NOTHING! John 3:16 says, "For God so loved...He gave," His best, His beloved, His unique, His only begotten Son!

All this the Servant, the Messiah *Yeshua/Jesus* has done for you, what have you ever done for Him? He died for you, so you could live for Him. He took your hell so you could take His heaven. What He suffered physically on *Mt Moriah* or Mt Calvary, on the tree or on the cross, whatever you want to call it, is nothing compared to what He suffered mentally, spiritually, internally.

It all started in the garden of the olive press, "Gethsemane" where He could feel the crushing weight of the sin of the world to come. So much so, that an angel from heaven was sent to strengthen Him, Lk. 22:43.

This is the only place in the KJV where the word 'agony' appears, Lk. 22:44 meaning, "to be engaged in combat." Who is He fighting? In Dan. 10:10-21, Daniel's prayer lasted 21 days until Gabriel was sent. (As angels are sent forth on behalf of the heirs of salvation, demons are sent forth on behalf of Satan's world system). He agonizes over what's in the cup, His

Father gave Him to drink. Yet He prays, "Not My will but, Thine be done." Mark 14:34 (He prayed that 3 times). It was here that Dr. Luke records the "Bloody Sweat" in Lk. 22:44 (*hematohidrosis*) under great stress your capillaries burst and mix with perspiration and you sweat blood, causing weakness, shock and even death!

According to Webster the word, 'Excruciating – to cause great agony, torment, and pain; comes from the Latin words, "Ex – for out of; and Cruciate – for cross; Or from or out of the cross. So, before the Carthaginians invented crucifixion and the Romans perfected it, the word 'Excruciating' wasn't even in the vocabulary.

Matt. 27:46 says, "And about the ninth hour (3:00 pm) Jesus cried with a loud voice, *"Eli, Eli, lama, sabach`thani?"* That is to say, 'My God, My God, why have You forsaken Me?" With the sin of the world pressing down upon Him Jesus suffered, 'Spiritual-Death' (Separation from the Father). Something you and I will never have to experience if we are saved! Isa. 59:2 says, 'Sin causes a separation from God, therefore He must turn His face from you, so that He cannot not hear you.' The father must turn away from His Son on the cross, He has no alternative!

So, for the first time, in recorded scripture anyway, Jesus does not address God as His Father! If you listen carefully, you can hear the internal plea in His external cry! This is the painstaking shrill of one who is in a state of utter loneliness! Can you hear it? It was for you and for me! *"Eli, Eli, la`ma, sabach`thani!"* Hab. 1:13; Isa. 1:15; Micah 3:4; Jer. 11:11; Ezk. 8:18; He doesn't address God as His Father at this moment, why? Because He became our sin offering!

Yeshua/Jesus had 'External-Warfare,' 'Internal-Warfare' and 'Spiritual-Warfare.' Psalm 22, "The Psalm of The Cross," talks about 'Spiritual-Warfare.' In vv. 12-13 it says, "Many bulls have compassed me; strong bulls of *Bashan* have beset me round. They gaped upon me with their mouths, like a ravening and a roaring lion."

While on the cross darkness that could be felt covered the land/earth Luke 23:44 from 12:00 – 3:00 p.m. *Yeshua/Jesus* associated those who arrested Him with the powers of darkness. Isa. 60:2 says, "For behold the darkness shall cover the earth and gross darkness (outer darkness) the peoples." Where were Satan and the powers of evil when Christ was on the cross? Ps. 22:12-13, seem out of place at first, but they have a deeper spiritual meaning upon further study which I am not going to go into here. However, I would challenge you to study further into the 'Bulls of Bashan,' Psalm 22, Og, the Rephaim, the Nephilim, the remnant of the giants, etc. In fact Spurgeon wrote a poem about Immanuel mentioning the 'Bulls of Bashan.' (See Endnote #2)

I Pet. 5:8 says, "Satan is a roaring lion, seeking whom he may devour." Bashan, is east of the Jordan River, known for its fertility; and tied too Baal and demon/spirit worship of cattle, giant cattle. These verses suggest the spiritual activity of Satan and demons celebrating the suffering of Jesus on the cross, their goal was to do away with Him once and for all! (Sorry Satan, but He is alive, He arose from the dead!)

We know from John 10:17-18 that Christ laid down His own life and that no man took it from Him; He had power to lay it down and power to take it up again. But physically and internally what was it that finished Him off? Exhaustion, thirst, asphyxiation, suffocation, dehydration, shock from blood loss, what? After He gave up His Spirit and the guards broke the legs of the other men and came to Christ they saw that He was already dead, but just to make sure, a soldier shoved a spear into His side and blood and water poured out.

Indicating the two most prominent causes of death probably were hypovolemic shock and exhaustion asphyxia. Others have proposed dehydration, cardiac arrhythmia and congestive heart failure with rapid accumulation of pericardial and pleural effusions as possible contributing factors, but Christ crying out with a loud voice rules out asphyxia. Put all that in layman's terms, He gave up His spirit and died from a 'broken heart' more like a 'ruptured heart.' Why? He took your place and was abandoned by His Father! **ABANDONED**!

The truth is, "He died for your sins!" According to the scriptures, I Cor. 15:3. The proof is, "He was buried Jewish style," I Cor 15:4: The truth is, "He arose from the dead!" According to the scriptures, I Cor. 15:4. The proof is, "He was seen above 500 brethren at once," I Cor. 15:6. The sufferings of our Messiah should always be the main subject on our hearts and minds, always, whether internal or external. "*ALL we* like sheep have gone astray; **We** have turned everyone to his own way, and the LORD has laid on **Him/Christ** the iniquity of us *ALL*."

Question? If Israel is the Servant, the **'Him'** that the LORD laid the iniquity on in the third phrase of this verse, "for the LORD has laid on Him/Israel the iniquity of us all" then who is the **'we'** in the first and second phrase that Isaiah identified himself with, the Goi'im, the Gentile nations, and that would make Isaiah a Gentile prophet, right because he is part of the we? *Hmmm?*

Chapter Four: The Servant Cut – Off (Isa 53:7-9)

Part One: The Servant's Illicit Arrest – Isa. 53:7

For almost 1,400 years, 'Passover Lambs' were killed pointing forward to 'Something.' Giving only a cryptic, silent witness of the (*owth*) in Exodus 12:13, a sign of something or someone greater to come. "And the blood shall be to you for a token (*owth* – sign of something greater to come) upon the houses where you are; and when I see the blood, I will pass over you." Now, 'That Someone,' 'That Something,' is finally revealed in Isaiah 53:7 and it is "The Servant, The Messiah" of Israel; "**He** was oppressed, and **He** was afflicted, yet **He** opened not **His** mouth; **He** is brought as a lamb to the slaughter, and as a sheep before her shearers is dumb, so **He** opened not **His** mouth." Isa. 53:7

From Isaiah 53:7 to John 1:29 in the Newer Testament there is but one single, solitary step! John the Baptizer is standing in the Jordan River baptizing people and he sees *Yeshua/Jesus of Nazareth* coming to him and he states, "Behold (*ide* – Look! Lo! See! Behold!), the Lamb of God, who takes away the sin of the world."

In Gen. 22:7-8 Abraham & Isaac are walking up Mt. Moriah and Isaac says, "My father, behold the fire and the wood, but where is the lamb for a sacrifice?" And Abraham said, "My son, God will provide Himself *(as)* a lamb for a burnt offering;" The word 'Himself' is a reflexive pronoun in the Hebrew text pointing back to God. In Jn. 8:56, *YeshuaJesus* said, "Abraham rejoiced to see My day and He saw it and was glad!" When did he see it? On Mt. Moriah, in the form of the 'Angel of LORD.'

By the way, Isaac never came down from the mountain, in v.19 it says, "Abraham returned to the two men and they returned to Beer-Sheba. You don't see Isaac again until he takes a bride in Gen. 24:62-67. (Sounds like a type of Yeshua/Jesus to me!)

We now come to the termination, the grand finale, or the consummation of the Servant! The (*coup de grace*) if you will, or the 'stroke of mercy!' As, Webster calls it, "The deathblow or shot, to end the suffering of one mortally wounded, a decisive finishing blow, act or event." In v. 7 we have, 'The Servant's Trial;' In v. 8, we have, 'The Servants Death;' And in v. 9 we have, 'The Servants Burial.' In this stanza we have the servant "Cut-Off!"

In this stanza the consequence of the sins of "All of us" fall on this Servant! All prearranged, preplanned, predetermined, preordained, before occurring, before creation, before time, before life, before light! In fact, it sounds more like history than prophecy! Hebrews 9:26 says, "For then must He often have suffered since (*apo* – from or before) the foundation of the world." (Who? The Messiah; The Servant, Heb. 9:24)

Again in Rev. 13:8 it says, "The Lamb slain before the foundation of the world." He didn't just suffer some minor affliction and suffering; He was executed even though he Himself was innocent! You need to get this! He took your Hell, so you could take His Heaven! '**He Took Your Place**!' You see, our salvation, our redemption, yours and mine, was not an afterthought of the Almighty, it was a forethought, it was pre-ordained, pre-planned!

Our sin did not catch Him by surprise or off guard! He knew all about Genesis 3! He knew Adam would sin and He created him anyway, now that's LOVE! He knew Eve was going to eat that pomegranate first. Real love is, an unconditional commitment, to an imperfect person and has nothing to do with feelings; it's all about an unconditional commitment, and an eternal covenant!

Isaiah 53:7 shows us the voluntary submission of the Servant of the LORD to a lost, hell bound dying world. It was His will to go to the tree, not because it was fun but because it had to be done. Salvation is free to us, but it cost Christ everything, including His life! It was preordained before the foundation of the world, as seen in, Mark 14:21, "The Son of man indeed goes as it is written of Him; but woe to that man by whom the Son of man is betrayed! Good were it for that man if he had never been born."

Speaking of Judas Iscariot, Judas means 'praised;' and Iscariot means man from *Kerioth* or 'the man of the assassins' so together his name means, "Praised man of the Assassins." Indwelt by Satan himself John 13:27 in the upper-room to carry out his diabolical plot. There was a council in heaven before the foundation of the world and the 'Servant' said, "I'll Go, I'll be the Lamb, the *Pascha*, The Sacrifice!" Acts 2:22-23; I Pet. 1:20. It is very important to note that it was at this verse, Isa. 53:7-8 that Philip lead the Ethiopian Eunuch to the Messiah, Acts 8:32 and it goes on to say that, "He preached unto to him *Jesus*."

So in the third stanza of our "Crown Jewel" Isaiah considers three consequences of having the sins of "All of us" fall on this Servant: 'Submissiveness, Injustice & Innocence:' This Servant was <u>submissive unto death</u> without a complaint like a butchered (*tebakh* – to kill ruthlessly) lamb! This Servant was <u>unjustly cut-off</u> *(karath)* due to other peoples sins, not His own! This Servant died and was buried even though <u>He was innocent</u>!

"He was oppressed, and He was afflicted, yet He opened not His mouth;" You have a very vivid contrast between v.6 where we all go astray – our own way and v.7 where this one sheep goes straight to the slaughter, His face set like flint, determined, destined, designed! Also interesting, you have the masculine singular pronoun <u>seven times</u> in this verse, <u>five times</u> as **He** and <u>twice</u> as **His**. Never once as a feminine plural to refer to a group of people such as Israel!

The word oppressed in Hebrew is (*na-gas*) meaning harshly treated and mishandled, or to drive, tax, tyrannize, distress, to be hunted or plagued, by a taskmaster or slave driver, Exodus 1 & 2. To sternly exact a penalty, payment, tribute or ransom! 'Full-Payment! 'He Paid The Debt In Full!' (Greek - *Tetelestai*! "It is FINISHED!")

"And He was afflicted," (*anah*) humbled, humiliated, to bow or stoop down, to mistreat, to dishonor; to ravish! This is the same word used in v. 4, "stricken, smitten, of God and afflicted," (*naga, naka, anah*) to describe His hell on earth for us, for you and me, as He bore our sin on the tree, yours and mine, all of it!

You can see this in the Newer Testament spelled out for us in Matt. 27:27-31; **(R)**; Mark 15:16-23; Luke 22:63-65; and John 19:1-3. He was oppressed (*nagas*) and afflicted (*anah*) driven, hunted, plagued, humiliated, humbled, mocked, and bowed down, for you because He loves you!

"Yet He opened not His mouth!" (Twice this is stated in this verse for emphasis) Why? Because v.10, He understood the 'Big Picture!' The larger purpose of God, seen in vv. 10-12; "The Servant Satisfied!"

Matt. 26:62-63, "And the high priest arose and said unto Him, Answerest thou nothing? What is it which these witness against thee? But *Yeshua/Jesus* held His peace." Matt. 27: 12-14, "And when He was accused by the chief priests and elders, He answered nothing. Then Pilate said unto Him, Hearest thou not how many things they witness against thee? And He answered him never a word..." Mark 15:1-5. Silence before the Elders; Silence before the Scribes; Silence before the Priests; Silence before the Pharisees; Silence before Herod and Pilate; **"SILENCE!"**

WHY? Silence can be deafening at times and this was one of them. **First**, He did not need to defend Himself because no valid accusation was made against Him. **Second**, His trial was a judicial farce conducted by men asserting pious motives who were violating the Jewish laws of jurisprudence, so I don't think any defense would have made any difference anyway! Do you? **Third,** His death sentence was predetermined and settled before they gave Him a hearing or a trial anyway, so what difference would it have made?

Fourth, He spoke to the Sanhedrin only when silence would have been a renunciation of His deity and His Messiahship, (Read) Matt. 26:63-64. "I adjure thee (*ex-or-kidzo*- to swear under oath or penalty of a curse) by the living God, that thou tell us if thou be the Christ, the Son of God! **Fifth,** He spoke before Pilate only when His silence would have renounced his kingship. Jn. 19:8-11 ® **Sixth,** However, before the incestuous Tetrarch Herod, He said nothing at all.

Now whatever virtues Israel has, and they have many, 'suffering silently' is not one of them nor ours. We tolerate pain and suffering, He embraced it (*yada*) became intimate with it, silently! In fact the Jewish people never considered suffering silently as a virtue, NEVER!

Take the 'Warsaw Ghetto' as an example, both of my grandparents grew up there before 1900. My grandmother's entire family was butchered in a pogrom and she had to be smuggled out of Poland by two Roman Catholic nuns. Why? She was Jewish!

What about the Palestinians, the Syrians, Hamas, the Hezbollah, etc. Is Israel suffering silently right now or are they fighting back, with all their might and military power? This Servant, is obviously a different character than the nation of Israel or any human being for that matter and Israel never, ever considered suffering silently as a virtue, **NEVER!**

"He is brought as a lamb to the slaughter;" A frequent symbol of the savior in Scripture! A lamb died for each Jewish family every year at "Passover;" Ex. 12:1-13; This servant died for His people – Israel Isa. 53:8; John 1:29, Yeshua/Jesus is the Lamb of God who takes away the sin of the world; 28 times in Rev. Yeshua/Jesus is referred to as "The Lamb."

He is Brought (*yabal*) borne, carried, led to the altar of sacrifice on Golgotha. This word is also a picture of pall bearers carrying someone to their grave. They are dead and silent, but this lamb is alive and silent. It is a lamb (*seh*) a lamb of the first year, a lambkin, just off its mother's milk. Lambs were sacrificed not sheep, they made no resistance, uttered no complaint.

A lamb provided no wool, no milk, not much meat so they were perfect for sacrifice because they were so innocent looking and provided no resistance! To the slaughter (*tebakh*) means to butcher or kill ruthlessly; although the Jewish people were very merciful in slaying their animals; Their butchers were not merciful in slaughtering them!

The *'shohet'* or Jewish butcher uses a 20" knife, highly polished, sharp as a razor, 2" wide, they cut the throat to sever the head so the animal feels little or no pain and death is quick. Lambs walk right up to their executioner and allow them to slit their throat but not cattle or other animals, they must be restrained, and locked in because they go wild at the smell of blood.

"And as a sheep before her shearers is dumb, so He opens not His mouth." As a sheep (*rachel*) a ewe-sheep, before her shearers is dumb (*alam*) this word means silent and bound all four legs. They usually tie their feet to shear them but the word (*alam*) can be translated to bind or binding. Either way they are silent during the shearing process. Matt. 27:2; Mark 15:1; John 18:12-13; 24. He was tormented, tortured, tried yet He opened not His mouth. He offers no defense, NONE! Just silence! Except when He is asked if He is God! Mark 14:61-62 and He answers in the affirmative (*ego eime*) "I am; the (*I AM*) and you shall see the Son of man sitting on the right hand of power, and coming in the clouds of heaven." (Dan. 7:13)

"Then the high priest rent his clothes (which was forbidden by the law except for blasphemy, Lev. 10:6; 21:10) and said, what need have we of any further witnesses? You have heard the blasphemy. What think ye? And they all condemned Him to be guilty of death."

The word shearers in Hebrew is a very interesting word (*gazaz*) to shear sheep or to shave one's head. We know in Isa. 50:6 it is believed that they ripped the Messiah's beard out, probably at this point by the roots. Is it possible that they also sheared His head, Isaiah 53:7 as a final act of humiliation before delivering Him to Pilate to scorn Him because He was thought to be a Nazarene from Nazareth and He may have taken a Nazarite vow, so they wanted to shame Him further?

Just a thought to give relevance to, "As a sheep before her shearers (*gazaz*) is dumb (*alam*) silent and bound;" In the movie, "The Lion, The Witch and the Wardrobe," when Aslan was on the stone altar just before the witch slew Him, they shaved His mane to humiliate Him one last time. (Maybe C.S. Lewis had a similar thought?) During the Holocaust the Nazi soldiers would cut off the Rabbi's beards publicly, in the streets to humiliate them and they sheared their heads in the concentration camps. (Just a thought but one worth considering).

The trial was totally illegal. It was illegal for the Temple guard to affect an arrest. It was illegal to try a capital charge (trial for life) at night; that was illegal. Only trials for money could be transacted after dark. It was illegal for judges to cross examine a prisoner after the testimony of the witnesses broke down, Matt. 26:57-68. In which case the prisoner was immediately released and the witnesses were immediately stoned.

Based on Deut. 16:18-20, the Jewish Court, the 'Bet Din' guaranteed a criminal several things: 1. A fair public trial; 2. A defense counsel; 3. Conviction only by the testimony of two witnesses; 4. A death sentence had to wait three days while the court members fasted and prayed; 5. A defendant was protected against self-incrimination; 6. A court officer rode in front of the defendant calling out for one witness to contradict the charges. No one stood up, not one of His disciples, followers, not even His own mother; No One!

In Matt. 26:57-68 we see at least six aspects of an illegal trial: **One** - Convening of the Sanhedrin at night, v. 57-58; **Two** - Conspiracy to convict without evidence, v. 59-61; **Three** - Confrontation for self-incrimination, v. 62-64; **Four** - Condemnation based on false testimony, v. 65-66; **Five** - Conduct of the court, verbal and physical abuse, v. 67-68. **Six** - The Servant's Response - 'Silence!' v. 67-68.

The Servant was brought to the shearers that He might be shorn of His honor, shorn of His majesty, shorn of His dignity, shorn of His glory, shorn of His power and shorn of His life. However, while the shearer's blades did their work, He was as silent as a lamb!

The Servant/Messiah wept and He sweat great drops of blood (*hematohidrosis*) but He never once murmured or felt rebellion in His heart, not one time! Not one syllable of complaint about His chastisement for our sins was ever uttered, never! How patient He was before Caiaphas, before Herod, before Pilate, before the crowd at Calvary. Silence! Never accusing them or us of injustice or cruelty, never! He just prayed, "Father, forgive them for they know not what they do!" Ten words that changed the philosophy of this world forever and ever!

We on the other hand murmur and cry out at any and every slight injustice thinking ourselves wrongly done by it, "I'll sue you for everything you have!" "You'll hear from my lawyer!" But not this 'Servant,' silent as a lamb to be slaughtered, silent as a sheep to be sheared, complete submission, complete self-sacrifice, complete self-conquest, complete self denial! (Luke 9:23)

He was oppressed, He was abased, He was afflicted, He was offered because he was willing; The idea is one of urgency, oppression, vexation, of being hard pressed, and ill treated. It does not refer to what was exacted by God or to sufferings inflicted by God, though it may include those. This refers to all of His oppressions and the severity of all His sufferings from everyone and from every area, physical, spiritual, human and demonic! He submitted Himself to be afflicted and yet He was as patient as a Lamb, as tender a newborn babe and He opened not His mouth! The idea here is that He voluntarily took upon Himself the sins of mankind, making Himself answerable as surety for the human race and that was the cause of His suffering. God demanded the debt be paid in 'FULL' and He the Great and Righteous One suffered to the full extent for it!

The KJV has retained the correct sense of the Hebrew in this verse, "He was <u>oppressed</u> and he was <u>afflicted</u>, yet He <u>opened not His mouth</u>!" He was subjected to excruciating pain and sorrow which was hard to bear; which was usually accompanied by expressions of impatience and lamentation! The fact that He never opened His mouth is even more remarkable & miraculous! He made no resistance; He uttered no complaint; You can almost see the patient Redeemer being led to Calvary without resistance, amidst the roar of the multitude yelling, "Crucify Him!" He is perfectly silent and composed, able to call 10,000 angels to assist Him in a nana-second; with all the power of heaven and earth at His disposal, yet quiet and gentle as if He had none; *He walked!*

Why? **'LOVE!'** "For God so loved the world that He gave His only begotten Son, that whosoever believes in Him should not perish, but have everlasting life." **Jn. 3:16**: "By this perceive we the love of God, because He laid down His life for us, and we ought to lay down our lives for the brethren." **I Jn. 3:16**; "And without controversy great is the mystery of godliness: God was manifest in the flesh, justified in the Spirit, seen of the angels, preached unto the nations, believed on in the world, received up into glory." **I Tim. 3:16**. "Then they that feared the LORD spoke often one to another; and the LORD <u>hearkened</u>, and <u>heard it</u> and a book of remembrance was written <u>before Him, for them</u> that feared the LORD, and that thought upon His name." **Mal. 3:16**.

PRAYER - "Father, just the title of this section, 'The Servant Cut-Off' (*gazar*) makes us tremble inside. To think that the Servant/Messiah went through all this for us because You loved us and He uttered not a word of rebellion or remorse. We know nothing of this kind of love but Thank

You, that You loved us that much; that before the foundations of the earth it was decided to send Your Son to be 'Cut-Off' so we wouldn't be! Thank You, in His glorious name we pray. Amen!"

****

Part Two: The Servant's Illegal Trial – Isa. 53:8

"He was taken from prison and from judgment; and who shall declare His generation? For He was cut off out of the land of the living; for the transgression of my people was He stricken." **K.J.V.**

"By oppression and judgment he was taken away, And with his generation who did reason? For he was cut off out of the land of the living, For the transgression of my people to whom the stroke was due." **JPS Trans. 1975.**

"By oppressive judgment he was taken away, Who could describe his abode? For he was cut off from the land of the living, Through the sin of my people, who deserved the punishment." **JPS Trans. 1985.**

He was snatched away from the earth, out of the midst of an atmosphere of prison and judicial proceedings. Out of His generation and all of his contemporaries and friends, who among them considered God's view, the true view of this criminal act? (No One! He's alone, Abandoned by everyone, including His father!)

Isaiah states, "He was snatched away out of the land of 'my people' to whom the stroke was rightfully due!" The emphasis in this verse is not that he was taken away from his sufferings but that, '**out of the midst of his sufferings he was carried off to death**!' That's the point of this verse! You need to catch that point!

Remember, 'IF' this Servant is the Messiah and not Israel; Which by now it is hard to argue for it being Israel, especially in this verse; And this Messiah is *Yeshua/Jesus* which it apparently seems to point too! Then *Yeshua* was arrested in the evening, which was against Jewish law except for money, had five or six trials by dawn, was beaten, buffeted (punched repeatedly), scourged, mocked, ridiculed, crowned with thorns, maybe two inches in length, stripped naked and executed by crucifixion and had a spear shoved into his side to make sure he was dead and buried in a borrowed tomb! Not very pretty for God's only unique Son, is it? So the second parallel to this enigma, seems to balance the first!

So, let's examine this illegal trial more closely, First: **"He was taken from prison and from judgment;"** To His death! He was taken (*la-kakh*) to seize, snatch, capture, carry away, take captive, to be taken prisoner in a hostile sense against your will and the will of others. (Peter the sword fighter, John 18:10, Malchus)

Think of the Garden of Gethsemane when *Yeshua/Jesus* was arrested in the night by the Temple guards who had no powers of arrest. NONE! They bound Him, seized Him and led Him away to Annas first to be tried. John 18:10ff. The father-in-law of Caiaphas which was also illegal.

Notice also the masculine singular pronouns 'He-Him-His' in this verse four times, seven times in v. 7 and four times in v. 9. Actually it appears over 50 times in this passage alone and 41 are personal pronouns!

"He was taken from prison" (*me-otzer*) this word is used only four times as a noun and means a place of confinement or violent oppression, and vengeance. (A very nasty word!) The root is to restrain, retain, or shut up, to imprison. It does not mean prison like our prisons today, it means a violent restraint and oppression; To be shut up and closed in, or confined.

"And from judgment," (*mish-pawt*) justice, court or the seat of judgment, or due process of litigation; this is a legal term, for a court room. His was an oppressive, unrighteous proceeding. Prison and justice refer to the judicial process or the due process of the law. He was taken from prison and from the very court room to be executed/terminated.

He suffered under the law and a sentence was passed in His case. The Hebrew Bible says, "By oppression and judgment He was taken or snatched away." He was condemned to die by legal execution, not by accident, old age, or by war, but by 'Legal Execution!' This is prophetic! Try to prophesy your death at the age of 33, in good health! (Try it! I dare you? I double dare you?)

This verse speaks of an illegal trial, no justice, no judgment; no one speaks on His behalf, no defense attorney, 'No One!' An oppressive, unrighteous proceeding, unethical and illegal! In fact He was sold for 30 pieces of silver Zech. 11:12-13; Matt. 26:15; The price of a gored, bleeding to death, slave, Exodus 21:32. ® It was called 'Blood Money.' Matt. 26:6-10.

"And who shall declare His generation," This is a tough passage to interpret and there are many variations, too many to cover here! So, I will take the one of a crier who went before a convicted criminal, with a flag in his hand calling for anyone to come forward to declare his innocence and the execution would be stopped and the trial retried, but no one, not John, not Peter, not even His mother stepped forward! This is recorded in the Babylonian Mishnah and Gemarah. In fact based on this passage the Gemarah of Babylon adds, "That before the death of *Yeshua/Jesus* this proclamation was made for 40 days but no defense could be found." (This is certainly false!)

However when you link v. 8 with v. 10, "Prolong His days and declare His generation." It appears to imply continuous posterity for all His generations even after being cut-off. In other words, He would win more disciples, more followers in His death than in His life. That's true for many believers. There are so many different opinions on this phrase it is unbelievable and they are all relevant and have their own valid arguments. But the indifference of the public opinion and apathetic attitude of the masses are often appalling, no one seemed concerned about His fate, as they cried, "Give us Barabbas!" Or "Give us 'Bar-Rabboni,' "The Son of The Rabbi!" I don't have the time or space to develop this one!

His judges were not interested in ascertaining the truth about their prisoner, just in getting rid of Him before the Sabbath. So, they could enjoy their Passover celebration! However, little thought was given to the importance of the death of *Yeshua/Jesus* by his contemporaries, life just went on; things were just too turbulent.

Except for His disciples and followers; and of course world history which was divided into two epochs, B.C. 'Before Christ' and A. D. 'Anno Domini' the year of our Lord Jesus Christ. Just pick up a news-paper, even in Russia and read the date! (Sunday – (vuhs-kree-syehn-yeh) "The day the Lord arose from the dead!" Try that for a witnessing tool!

Nothing seemed to change, and yet everything seemed to change: the veil was rent, rocks were rent, graves were rent, hearts were rent, history was rent, Jerusalem was rent, Judaism was rent, Rome was rent, the world was rent, Hell was rent, and Heaven was ripped wide open! The day they crucified Christ!

"For He was cut-off out of the land of the living;" The word cut-off (*gaw-zar*) is a special Hebrew word used only six times in the Bible. It means to be cut down, destroyed, killed, exterminated, executed and refers to a violent horrible death! This is a special word used for the execution of criminals. This is a violent, shocking death, never a peaceful death, one that turns your head and stomach. This is the kind of death they would date things from, like 'Pearl Harbor 12/7/41;' the 'Kennedy Assassination 11/22/63;' the 'Twin Towers 9/11/01;' the 'Atomic Bombs 8/6/9/45 – Hiroshima & Nagasaki – "Little Boy & Fat Man"

This is the first time Scripture indicates that the Messiah would die, and die a horrible, violent, ugly death; up to this point it just said that He would suffer, but never die! The normal word for cut-off (*karath*) is used over 200 times in the Bible and means to be condemned to eternal Hell fire or 'Eliminated!' Dan. 9:26, "And after threescore and two weeks shall Messiah be **cut off** but not for Himself; and the people of the prince that shall come shall destroy the city and the sanctuary, and the end of it shall be with a flood, and unto the end of the war desolations are determined." This word is a special word (*gaw-zar*) and means 'Exterminated **NOT** Eliminated!' Which is very important! (A very strong word, to cut in two with an axe, to cut down in the midst of his days).

He was also cut-off from life prematurely maybe 33.5 years up to maybe 38 years. If, He was born in 5 B.C. prior to Herod's death and died in 33 A.D. which many Bible scholars hold to, that would make Him about 37-38 years old. He lived a short life, dying in His prime, but His impact on men's hearts and lives had only just begun. He had no successor, no family, no descendants to preserve His name. He came and ministered for 3.5 years and died.

However, He can't be erased from the consciousness or souls of the human race, no matter how hard or how long they try. He may have been cut-off out of the land of the living but He will never be cut-out of the hearts, souls and spirits of those He left behind, Never! They may be able to take the tree out of the malls, and the manger out of the halls, but they will never take Christ out of Christmas! All history is based on His birth and eternity on His death!

"For the transgression of 'My' people was He stricken." Some translators believe that YeHoVaH is speaking in this verse and that the word "My" should be capitalized. It also needs to be pointed out that this servant is not carried off and executed due to an illegal, corrupt system, but because of, "the transgressions of My people." (That's Very Imp!)

He is suffering in the place of those who should be suffering, and He dies the death they should be dying! It was not His death on false charges that saved the world! It was His voluntary submission as the infinite God-Man, to bear the sins of the world and die on the cross of Calvary that made Him the Savior of all mankind. Col. 1:13-14; 19-20. The (*pesh-ah*) transgression, trespasses, rebellion, revolts, or crossing the line.

Wilson's Old Testament word studies says, "This is a strong word meaning to rebel against (*YHWH*) or Jehovah, to apostatize from Him or against Him. To revolt or rebel or to be lawless, whether it is national or individual; moral or religious rebellion. The Hebrews used six nouns and three verbs to describe sin, but the three main ones are; (***Pesah***) crossing the line, rebellion, or transgression: (***Aw-von***) iniquity, perverse, twisted, or crooked: (***Chet***) omission, or missing the mark.

"For the transgression (*Pesh-ah*) of my people; (*am - nation*)" Who are Isaiah's people? Israel, then how can the Servant be Israel if He is going to be cut-off (*gaw-zar*) exterminated for Isaiah's people? (He can't be – Right?) That doesn't take rocket science to figure out! Oh, you can twist the grammer and corrupt the syntax, but dead still means, DEAD!

The word stricken (*ne-ga*) is the same word as in v. 4, to strike violently, to kill, to slaughter, or to strike fatally. The Hebrew Scriptures read, "For the transgression of my people to whom the stroke was due!" Or, "Through the sin of my people, who deserved the punishment!" David,

Moses, Joseph, Isaiah even Israel didn't die for Israel, they couldn't. (But they deserved the punishment or the stroke!) You had to be sin-less to be a sin-offering, as you can see in v. 10. You also had to be the infinite *God-Man* to suffer the infinite wrath of Almighty God and Israel was neither.

The Servant in this passage cannot be; I repeat, cannot be Israel! How could Israel be cut-off (*gawzar*) exterminated for Israel and still be a nation today? Impossible! It makes no sense! There is reason to believe that the original text of this phrase has been changed. The ancient text seems to have stated, **"He was smitten unto death."** Or, **"Stricken to death!"**

The Septuagint LXX has, "because of the iniquities (lawlessness) of my people He was led to death!" The Greek word for law is (*nomos*) and the word for lawless is (*a-nomos*). Nomos is the Law, the Torah according to Paul & John and living without it is (*a-nomos*) sin! Nomos with the alpha privative to negate it! The original word in the Hebrew text was probably (*lama-veth*, intensive plural, violent death) but it was changed, sometime after 200 ad to (*lamo*) probably by the Mazorites.

That is the way it was written by Origen 185-254, who stated a certain Jewish person assured him of that translation and felt it was more accurate than any other part of Isaiah 53. It is rendered that way in the Septuagint in our present copies and if it wasn't that way in the original then it wouldn't be that way in the Septuagint, dated 250 B.C. Or in Origen's writings, or in the Jewish man's arguments: "The Messiah, Jesus the Christ, was smitten unto death!" For our transgressions, our rebellions, our trespasses, our sins, yours and mine!

"Origen," (Contra Celsum, lib. i. p. 370, edit. 1733,) after having quoted at large this prophecy concerning the Messiah, "tells us, that having once made use of this passage in a dispute against some that were accounted wise among the Jews, one of them replied, that the words did not mean one man, but one people, the Jews, who were smitten of God and dispersed among the Gentiles for their conversion; that he then urged many parts of this prophecy to show the absurdity of this interpretation, and that he seemed to press them the hardest by this sentence, "for the iniquity of my people was he smitten to death."

"Now as Origen, the author of the Hexapla, must have understood Hebrew, we cannot suppose that he would have urged this last quotation as so decisive if the Greek Version had not agreed here with the Hebrew text; nor that these wise Jews would have been at all distressed by this quotation, unless their Hebrew text had read agreeably to, "to death," on which the argument principally depended; for, by quoting it immediately, they would have triumphed over him, and reprobated his Greek version. This, whenever they could do it, was their constant practice in their disputes with the Christians."

"Jerome, in his Preface to the Psalms, says, "Lately disputing with a Hebrew,-thou advanced certain passages out of the Psalms which bear testimony to the Lord the Saviour; but he, to elude thy reasoning, asserted that almost all thy quotations have an import in the Hebrew text different from what they had in the Greek.""

"And Origen himself, who laboriously compared the Hebrew text with the Septuagint, has recorded the necessity of arguing with the Jews from such passages only as were in the Septuagint agreeable to the Hebrew: Wherefore as Origen had carefully compared the Greek version of the Septuagint with the Hebrew text, and speaks of the contempt with which the Jews treated all appeals to the Greek version where it differed from their Hebrew text; and as he puzzled and confounded the learned Jews by urging upon them the reading, "unto death," in this place; it seems almost impossible not to conclude, both from Origen's argument and the silence of his Jewish adversaries, that the Hebrew text at that time actually had (*lemaveth*) "to death," agreeably to the version of the Septuagint." Dr. Kennicott.

Basically, Origen would not have stood and debated with these Jewish Scholars if the Hebrew text and the Greek text were not in perfect agreement in his day, so someone changed the text! Don't get me wrong, Origen was responsible for much of the Anti-Semitism all of which was based on his assertion that the Jews were responsible for killing Jesus.

So, this Servant, Israel's Messiah; Who had to come before the destruction of the Temple 2,000 years ago; Do many wonderful miracles to authenticate His office, be a direct descendant of King David, have proof of His lineage in print even today; (Only in Matt. 1 and Luke 2.) Must have been born of a miraculous birth to avoid the sin nature of Adam and the sin curse of Jeconiah, Jer. 22:24-30; Be the Son in Isaiah 7:14 fulfilling the eight names in Isaiah 9:6 the *Midrash* talks about; Fulfilling over 300 prophecies in His birth alone; Who would be not only the Son-of-man and die to pay the penalty for mankind's sin but be the ultimate sacrifice to *YaHWeH* satisfying His holy demands, and rise from the grave on the third day victorious over death as the Son-of-God to reign as the King of kings and LORD of lords; And come back to reign and rule His kingdom for 1,000 years! Now if that is not *Yeshua/Jesus,* then you tell me who in time, space and history that is? And while you are searching through all your grey matter for someone, I'll put all my chips of the Man from Galilee, Jesus of Nazareth!

PRAYER - "Father, just saying the words "Cut-Off" (Exterminated) grieves our hearts and souls. But we know if He didn't die, we couldn't live; If He didn't suffer, we couldn't know healing; If He didn't know emptiness and loneliness and pain; We wouldn't know fullness and comfort and joy; If He didn't drink that cup, then we would have had too! **Thank You**, Father for sending the Servant, Your Son, the Messiah, *Yeshua ha Mashiach*, to die for us, so we could live for Him, one day at a time; Teach us to live, each day for Christ, as though it were our last. In *ha shem Yeshua's name we pray, Amen!"*

****

Part Three: The Servant's Illogical Burial – Isa. 53:9

"And he made his grave with the wicked, and with the rich in his death (intensive plural) because he had done no violence, neither was any deceit in his mouth." KJV

"And they made his grave with the wicked, And with the rich his tomb; Although he had done no violence, Neither was any deceit in his mouth." Isaiah 53:9, JPS Trans. 1955.

Actually the verb (made) is an impersonal, passive and is very important, "they **made**, appointed, or **assigned** his grave with the wicked." The wicked, evil, blasphemers, robbers, malefactors, mobsters, gangsters were not buried; they were cast on the garbage dump for the animals to devour, in the Valley of Hinnom, (Heb – Ge-Hinnom; Grk Ge-Henna) destination of the wicked. *Yeshua/Jesus* used this word 11 times in the Newer Testament, Mark 9:44-48. The Jewish leaders planned to disgrace Him as was their custom for, *'persona non grata'* for an unwelcome person. (Latin for 'An Unwelcome Person').

Josephus wrote in 'Antiquities of the Jews,' "He that blasphemes God, let him be stoned and let him hang upon a tree all that day and then let him be buried in an ignominious (despicable, disgraceful, shameful, dishonorable) and obscure manner." Matt. 26:65, "Then the high priest tore his clothes, saying, He has spoken blasphemy! What further need have we of witnesses? Behold, now ye have heard his blasphemy." They made plans for his body, to bury it with the wicked, but God had other plans!

The Newer Testament speaks nothing of these plans, thus confirming the inspiration of the Scriptures and allowing the Older Testament to illuminate the Newer Testament. After His death, the Messiah was buried in a rich man's tomb which is written in the Jewish Scriptures, Isaiah 53:9 which was obviously part of God's plan but not part of the Jewish leaders plan at that time but all four Gospels record this event.

"And he/they made His grave with the wicked," And **'They'** (plural) made His grave with the wicked (*resha'im*) plural, 'ungodly, wicked men.' He was crucified with criminals so He could be buried with them, that was the law. In fact the most wicked or the greatest offender was always put in the middle. The word made (*nathan*) means, to give, assign, appoint, set up, dedicate, or designate. So they assigned or designated His grave with the wicked, evil, ungodly (*rasha'im*) criminals.

These were guilty men, hostile to God and man, and after their execution their bodies were dragged out of town and thrown on the garbage heap for the rats and rodents to consume. Except for the sin of, 'Blaspheme.' For that crime a grave was dug in the valley of Ge-*Hinnom*, the garbage dump and polluted with pig's blood. The executed victim was then buried in it with his cross member to bear his shame *(olam)* for eternity. "Humanity vented its spleen in vicious treatment of God's Holy One." They held nothing back! However, after that spear pierced Messiah's side, nothing but hands of love would ever touch His body again and God the Father would make sure of that! Yeshua/Jesus had a Joseph at His birth and at His death!

The priests wanted His body, so they could bury it in the <u>assigned grave</u> and pleaded with Pilate for it, but his wife (Claudia) also interceded on the Messiah's behalf. Matt. 27:19. Joseph of Arimathaea a very rich man and Nicodemus a Pharisee, a ruler of the Jews, a master teacher of Israel and a very powerful man also pleaded for His body and they won Pilate's approval after the Centurion's testimony, Mark 15:39, "Truly this was the son of God."

Normally a criminal's death would warrant a criminal's grave, dragged out of the city and thrown on the garbage dump for animals and worms to consume. However, God intervenes and honors this Servant because His death was substitutionary and His life, totally sinless. Psalm 16:10 says, "For Thou wilt not leave my soul in *sheol*, (O.T. place of the departed, in other words he will be resurrected) neither wilt Thou permit Thine Holy One to see corruption (*sha-chat* – decay; he'll be in that grave a very short time, probably less than 40 hrs?)."

"And (but/yet) with the rich in His death;" The JPS, translation says; "And with the rich His tomb." His grave was appointed or assigned and polluted with pig's blood in the garbage dump in the valley of *Hinnom* with the criminals!

Gehenna is a place in the valley of *Hinnom* where in ancient times human sacrifices were offered (2 Chron. 33:6; Jer 7:31) and where continuous burning of rubbish illustrated for the Jewish people, unending punishment of the wicked, mostly children alive. This word occurs in Matt. 5:22, 29, 30; 10:28; 18:9; 23:15, 33; Mk. 9:43, 45, 47; Lk. 12:5 and Jam. 3:6. In every instance except one the word was spoken by *Yeshua/Jesus* in the most solemn warning of the consequences of sin. He described it as the place where, "the worm never dies and the fire is never quenched." Mk. 9:44. The expression is identical in meaning to the "lake of fire" Rev. 19:20; 20:10;

However, He would be buried in a rich man's tomb, how ironic! Now there is a Hebrew paradox or oxymoron! With the rich (*asir*) a wealthy person, how wealthy? Very wealthy! Well, the Jewish Encyclopedia identifies a Nicodemus Ben Gorion as a wealthy, respected member of the 'Peace Party' of the first century who had miraculous powers.

Then you have Joseph of Arimathaea whose unfinished garden tomb was given to the Messiah to be buried in and never used again. NEVER! Then you have the wrapping in fine linen and 100 pound weight of spices; myrrh and aloes. Myrrh cost about $400.00 a pound at that time, so 100 pounds of spices cost over $40,000.00. Take it down to our weight of 75 pounds and you still have over $30,000.00.

However, Nicodemus came to *Yeshua/Jesus* by night in John 3, then he stood up to defend Him in John 7, but in John 19 he is pleading for His body in public in daylight, before witnesses. Then he buries the body at a great cost and that cost was his position in the Sanhedrin as a Pharisee, and his position and privilege in the Temple and community as 'The Master Teacher' in Israel and a ruler among the Jewish people. John 3:10, "Jesus answered, and said unto him, "Art thou the master/teacher of Israel and knowest not these things?" The (*ha didaskalos*) this word implies authority over his followers and is used of Jesus in John 4:31; 8:4; 9:2; 11:8; 13:13; 20:16 etc. The cost of influence and affluence was probably far greater to Nicodemus than the cost of silver and gold was to Joseph of Arimathaea.

"In His death," (*ma-veth*) death by violence as a penalty and it is an intensive plural, **"deaths!"** This form emphasizes severe intensity and suggests a death so unthinkable that it is to be compared with dying again, and again, and again, and again... God uses the same word speaking to the Prince of Tyre in Ezek. 28:10, "Thou shalt die the **deaths** of the uncircumcised by the hand of strangers, for I have spoken it, saith the Lord GOD." Again, in Jer. 16:4 the LORD speaking to Jeremiah concerning Judah says, "They shall die of grievous **deaths**; they shall not be lamented, neither shall they be buried, but they shall be as dung upon the face of the earth;" (Doesn't sound very pleasant!)

Today we would call this dying a "thousand deaths!" But He died billions of deaths! Just another glimpse into the infinite bitterness of the cup of Almighty God's wrath the Messiah lifted with both hands in the garden and drank to the very dregs for all mankind. There could be no accidental fulfillment of such a prediction! He was executed between two criminals, to make sure He would have a criminal burial, that was the law, and He was buried in a rich man's tomb. This was all foretold 700 years before it literally happened, what are the chances?

"Because/Although He had done no violence, neither was any deceit in His mouth." The Hebrew Bible uses the word, **'Although'** which gives a better emphasis to this phrase; "Although (Even Though) He had done no violence (*hamas*) wrong, damage, injustice, unrighteousness, cruelty, malice;" He had done nothing wrong, in other words, He was innocent! "Neither was any deceit (*mirma*) deception, dishonesty, treachery, guile, falsehood or craftiness in His mouth." ("when selfish evil tries to masquerade as justice it prepares its own unmasking")

This Servant spoke only the Truth and nothing but the Truth, in fact He was the Truth, John 14:6. Peter in the Newer Testament verifies this prophecy in I Peter 2:22 speaking of the Messiah, "Who did no sin, neither was guile found in His mouth." Again Peter verifies His innocence in I Peter 1:19, "But with the precious blood of *Mashiach*, as of a lamb (*amnos* – lambkin) without blemish and without spot." Without blemish (*amomos*) faultless, unblamable, perfect; Complete innocence; He committed no crime in word, thought or deed. He was perfect! And without spot *(aspilos)* spotless, irreproachable, unsullied and unspotted!

This Servant was given an honorable burial after His dishonorable death because of His perfect honorable innocence, that's what it says, PERIOD! Pilate's wife called Him a 'Just Man' Matt. 27:19; Pilate called Him a 'Just Person' Matt. 27:24 and said, "I find no fault in Him." The thief hanging next to Him said, "This man has done nothing amiss." "Then answered all the people" and they made a profound statement or self judgment, "His blood be upon us and on our children." Matt. 27:25.

Here is this Servant, Israel's Messiah, innocent and devoid of guile or deceit. Oppressed; Tried Illegally; Humiliated; Arrested Illicitly; and Brutally Slaughtered! How does he respond? Listen to His complaining, His whining, His gripping, His belly aching, His grumbling and He certainly had reason for all of it! LISTEN….Do you hear anything? You mean, He is not complaining, demanding His rights, a fair trial, a good Jewish lawyer, clean sheets, a drink, a phone call, an appeal? NO! Silence!

However, the Messiah does speak eight times in fact and eight is the number for the Messiah. "The Eight Sayings from The Cross:" **One** - Luke 23:34, "Father forgive them for they know not what they do." (Ten Words that changed the philosophy of the world for all time) Matt. 27:46; **Two** - "My God, My God, why hast Thou forsaken Me?" (Nine Words – The only time He addressed God 'NOT' as His Father) Luke 23:43; **Three** - "Today shalt thou be with Me in paradise." (Eight Words – One sinner was saved so that no one would despair but only one so that no one would pre-suppose we would all make it) Luke 23:46; **Four** - "Father into Your hands I commend My spirit." (Eight Words – Trichotomy vs Dichotomy, His spirit went to the Father, His body went into the grave and His soul went to paradise, I Thess. 5:23; Heb. 4:12;) **Five** - John 19:26, "Woman, behold thy son!" (Four Words – I believe He was talking to His mother and she couldn't recognize Him, it was just a slab of meat, Isa. 52:14, no form, no visage, soo marred); **Six** - John 19:27, "Behold thy mother!" (Three Words - To the disciple whom He loved, He gave John charge of His mother, only she believed in Him); **Seven** – John 19:28, "I thirst!" (He received the vinegar, but not the first one with the gall Matt. 27:34 to numb the pain); **Eight** – "John 19:30, "It is finished! One word in Greek!" (The work of salvation is over, you can't add to it or detract from it, you can only accept it or reject it, but not accepting Him is the same as rejecting Him!

You know in light of the cross and all that Israel's Messiah has done for you and me, isn't it a shame you and I live the way we do? Such paltry, cheap, shabby, pitiful lives? Doing just enough to get by, giving just enough to appease our conscience. Do you give enough to get by or do you get by so you can give enough? It makes a 'BIG' difference, doesn't it?

Philosophers say, "If a virtuous man would come along the world would look up to him and follow him." Socrates said, "Nay my friend, he would be hated, despised, persecuted and killed!" What a coincidence! And as my Rabbi says, "Coincidence is not a Kosher word!"

So, what should our reaction be to all of this? **First** – Faith in His sacrifice; **Second** – Imitation of His example; **Third** – Remembrance of His love; **Fourth** – Exaltation of His glory!

Don't you think it's time we moved to the victory side of the tree and stopped our belly aching, whining, complaining and our pity parties? Don't you? This Servant, bankrupted heaven for us and we throw in our two bucks and feel we did our part! Shame on us!

Charles Wesley said, "If you doubt Christ's claims are real, you need to sit next to a dying Christian and a dying atheist just one time in your life and you will be convinced He is who He claimed to be!" Just one time, and watch them die, and listen to their final words! They are usually the same, ***"Oh my God!"*** One as they realize they have been wrong all their life; The other as they realize they have been right all their life! One is a cry of elation, euphoria, rapture and eternal life; The other is a cry of despair, doom, despondency and eternal damnation!

How could a prophet, 700 hundred years before an event, predict that one would be executed as a malefactor, with other malefactors, to be buried with them; then predict that he would be rescued from such a despicable, humiliating burial by the intervention of a rich man and be buried in a grave designated for a man of influence in the manner in which the wealthy are buried! **Absurd!** This was not some accident in history, a mistake made by misinformed leadership; of an innocent man, in the wrong place, at the wrong time, Who was executed by mistake!

This Servant's purpose in living, dying and offering Himself as a sinless sacrifice, was in order that through Him you and I might have our sins atoned for that we might come to know (*yada*) God on an intimate level and be made righteous in His sight! II Cor. 5:21.

As one author put it, "Only when people make a sin offering of Him (The Servant) is the point of this whole operation realized; then He (God) can breathe a sigh of satisfaction (*saba*)." Isa. 53:11. He also stated, "As a result of all this one day; This distorted, ignored, crushed Son of Man will wear a victor's wreath and all the other victors will throw theirs down at His feet." **Hallelujah!** *"And they assigned His grave with the wicked, and with the rich His tomb..." Isa. 53:9a, JPS*

Chapter Five: The Servant Satisfied (Isa 53:10-12)

Part One: The Servant's Soul Suffers – Isa. 53:10

"The Lord also is pleased to purge him from his stroke. If ye can give an offering for sin, your **soul** shall see long-lived seed:" Septuagint Version, (Lxx) Sir Lancelot Brenton.

"Yet it pleased the LORD to crush him by disease; To see if his **soul** would offer itself in **restitution**; That he might see his seed, prolong his days, And that the purpose of the LORD might prosper by his hand." Isa. 53:10, JPS Trans. 1975.

"Yet it pleased the LORD to bruise him; he has put him to grief. When thou shalt make his **soul** an offering for sin, he shall see his seed, he shall prolong his days, and the pleasure of the LORD shall prosper in his hand." KJV Trans. 1967.

You see, "The Servant Exalted" in Isaiah 52:13-15; "The Servant Despised" in Isaiah 53:1-3; "The Servant Wounded" in Isaiah 53:4-6; "The Servant Executed" in Isaiah 53:7-9; And now "The Servant Satisfied" in Isaiah 53:10-12, or 'The Satisfaction of The Servant' or 'The Servant Satisfies God's Holy demands for Sin.'

In v.10 we see the Servant's Resurrection; In v.11 we will see the Servant's Justification; And in v.12 we will see the Servant's Imputation. In this last portion you will also see the Servant's continued mediatorship in heaven as well as His continued efficacious sacrifice. This song began on a victory note in Isa. 52:13 and it will end on that same note in Isa. 53:12.

"Yet it pleased the LORD to bruise Him; He has put Him to grief." It pleased or delighted the LORD (*YHWH*) Jehovah, the God of Redemption to bruise Him; To utterly crush Him, (*daw-kaw*) to break or beat Him into pieces, to shatter Him. This is the same word you have in v. 5, "He was bruised for our iniquities;" crushed like a worm under your foot on the sidewalk. This is a brutal word, to crush, beat, stamp, and pulverize into dust.

It is used six times in the Older Testament and only once in the Newer Testament in Rom. 16:20, "And the God of peace shall bruise Satan under your feet shortly. The grace of our Lord Jesus Christ be with you. Amen!" Oh how God hates sin, Amen? How much do you hate it? I John 1:9.

The word pleased here, does not mean that the LORD was emotionally delighted in the Servant's suffering. I don't think the LORD, *YeHoVaH* is delighted emotionally when we suffer; Glorified Yes! Delighted - Never! Rom. 8:18 says, "For I reckon that the sufferings of this present time are not worthy to be compared with the glory which shall be revealed in us." (Wow! Brood on that for a while!). When the word 'pleased' is used in this way it's clearly referring to the LORD's will and purpose being fulfilled. This is judicial satisfaction of the law, and of God's holiness, and it had to be satisfied or we would all go to hell without exception!

"He (God) has put Him (Christ the Messiah) to grief (*hala*)." In the 'Dead Sea Scrolls' the word grief is translated "Pierced," to be mortally wounded (1 Q Is.). Franz Delitzch says, "It pleased *YeHoVaH* to smite Him painfully." In short, God permitted this outrage! In Isaiah 1:11-15 Isaiah said, "God had no pleasure in burnt offerings, sacrifices and incense; they were a vain oblation and an abomination to Him!" Why? His holiness wasn't being satisfied! (Read it)

You see, the LORD *YeHoVaH* was responsible for the Servant's death, not the Jewish people, not the Roman's, not the Gentile's. Only God Himself is qualified to provide salvation. Amen? He's had it with the Jewish people and their religious rituals! How about us and ours?

So, the Servant's death was not accidental or man made! In fact it was preplanned before the foundation of the earth: Acts 2:23, "Him being delivered by the <u>determinate counsel</u> and <u>foreknowledge</u> of God;" I Peter 1:20 says, "Who verily was <u>foreordained</u> before the <u>foundation of the world</u>;" Rev. 13:8 says, "And all that dwell upon the earth shall worship him (the beast v.1, 2, 3, 4) whose names are not written in the book of life of the Lamb slain from <u>the foundation of the world</u>."

Ps. 113-114 are sung at the beginning of Passover and Ps. 115-118 are sung at the end. Psalm 118:22-24 says, "The stone which the builders refused is become the head of the corner. This is the LORD's doing, it is marvelous in our eyes. This is the day which the LORD has made; we will rejoice and be glad in it." (We sing that chorus today--). This Day, refers to Calvary and the Cross. God did not go around it or circumvent it and neither can we. *Yeshua/Jesus* says, 'You have to go to the Tree to get to Me!' Col. 2:14 states, "Blotting out the handwriting of ordinances that was against us, which was contrary to us, and (He) took it out of the way, nailing it to His cross."

God's divine plan for redemption not only included the blood of animals to **'Cover'** sin Lev. 17:11, but also a permanent plan to remove sin forever, **'FORGIVENESS!!' Through His blood!** Study Hebrews chapter 10 in the Newer Testament sometime, it is such an amazing chapter, v. 4 says, "For it is not possible that the blood of bulls and of goats should take away sins." And it certainly is not *'Tashlikh'* (casting off) on *Rosh Hashanah*, Micah 7:19; Then how? The LORD appointed the Servant's soul to be an 'Offering for Sin.'

"When Thou shalt make His soul an offering for sin," A trespass offering, an (*a-sham*) a guilt offering, a compensating payment. This is the only direct mention in all of the Scriptures where the Messiah was specifically stated to be our <u>trespass-offering</u>! An (*a-sham*) was distinct from all other sacrifices; it was made by the individual for any wrong he had done. It released him from guilt, set him free and made full compensation, Lev.5:15-16.

The idea is satisfaction demanded by God's Holiness and **restitution** required by God's law. To be a Sin-offering you had to be Sin-less, perfect in every way, not one blemish (*amomos*) without spot, that was the requirement. Does Isaiah 1:4-6 sound like perfection when speaking of Israel? (Read it!) Then how could they be the Servant and thus the trespass-offering?

The Jewish Bible uses the word 'Restitution' which is full, total compensation. Sold to pay the full debt, to the last farthing! In Greek, the word is (*tetelestai*) paid in full, that was the 8th saying of *Yeshua/Jesus* from the tree, John 19:30; "It is Finished!" Or more appropriately,

"FINISHED!!" Propitiation is a $10.00 Greek word that basically means, 'Satisfying Sacrifice.' It appears four times in the N.T. twice as the means of propitiation (*hilasmos*) I John 2:2; 4:10 and twice as the place of propitiation (*hilasterion*) Rom. 3:25 and Heb. 9:5. (A very interesting study!)

The word atonement in Hebrew (*ka-far*) basically means to cover, to coat, to cover with pitch, to pacify, appease, to forgive, to atone for. However, it was never intended to 'Remove Sin,' never! Only to cover and pacify temporarily! (Like a nuk/pacifier for a newborn waiting for their bottle). The idea is not that the sinner offers up the Servant's soul but that the Messiah offers up His own soul as a 'Trespass Offering!' An (*a-sham*) to make full, complete restitution, full compensation, once and for all! For Us! How beautiful is that? And you think you got cheated, because you didn't get that promotion!

The Hebrew word for 'Restitution' is (*salem*) and can be translated, "It is finished, completed, fulfilled, paid in full!" Just like, John 19:30 – (*tetelestai*). II Cor. 5:21 says, "For He (God) has made Him (Christ) who knew no sin, to be sin for us, that we might be made the righteousness of God in Him." (Right Standing Before God!) What does that mean? To be made sin for us? Can you fathom that? A holy, pure, righteous, sinless, God being made sin! Can you? I certainly can't! What do we know about sin and about the effect it would have on the soul of a perfectly sinless person, especially if that person was the, 'Son of God? <u>Absolutely Nothing</u>!

Now you know why he prayed three times in the 'Garden of The Olive Press' for the cup to be removed and why He sweat great drops of blood (*hematohidrosis*). Not like blood, BLOOD! In Matt. 26:38 He said, "My soul is exceedingly sorrowful, even unto death; tarry here and watch with Me." Why? His soul is about to be made a 'Trespass Offering' and He is 'Exceedingly Sorrowful' (*peril-oo-pos*) even unto death, overcome with sorrow, so much so as to cause one's death! **Wow!**

I am having trouble wrapping my mind around this. Matt. 20:28 helps to reinforce this truth, "He came to give His life a ransom for many." Ransom (*lu-tron*) to fully pay the price to redeem. "<u>To make full restitution</u>." The JPS translation, got it right! "To see if his soul would offer itself in restitution! WOW!!

You see it was not just the physical suffering that made propitiation for our sin, but what He also endured in His holy, spotless, pure, sinless soul when it became our sin-offering. That's why the cry from Psalm 22:1, "My God, My God, why hast Thou forsaken Me?" (*Eli, Eli, lama sabach'thanai?* Matt. 27:46). He was forsaken, that we might be received, He was abandoned so we would never have to be! This is the only time in recorded Scripture when He referred to God, **not** as His Father! Isa. 53:10, 11, and 12 all refer to the 'soul' (*neph-esh*) of this Servant, Israel's Messiah!

His trespass offering produced three eternal results: **One - He shall see His seed; Two - He shall prolong His days; Three - The pleasure of the LORD shall prosper in His hand."** *First*, "He shall see His seed;" He shall see His posterity, His numerous spiritual offspring, you and me! Some Rabbi's say, "This can't refer to the Messiah's off-spring and especially *Yeshua/Jesus* because He never had any children." Read the context Rabbi, this verse specifically says the offspring will follow His death and therefore must refer to spiritual children. (Cut-off - *ga-zar* - v. 8; deaths - *ma-veth* - v. 9) Also compare John 12:24; Heb. 2:10-13; Isa. 9:6; Ps. 22:30; Isa. 65:25; Mal. 2:15.

Second, "He shall prolong His days;" He shall live long days; For He shall live by dying, John 12:24; Isa. 9:6 refers to Him as, '*Abbi Ad*,' Father of Eternity. The Midrash says, 'The son in Isaiah 7:14 is the same son in Isaiah 9:6 with eight names.' In their Tenach/Bible they transliterate them, they don't translate them, they are too Holy, "Pele; Joez; El; Gibbor; Abi; Ad; Sar; Shalom;" So if those are eight names for God, then the Son in Isa.7:14, the one born of a virgin, must also be God, Emmanuel, "God with us." A strange paradox, the Servant dies yet God will prolong His days. In Rev. 1:18, *Yeshua/Jesus* says, "I am He that lives and was dead and behold I am alive for evermore, Amen;" His resurrection, ascension and exaltation are all in view in v. 10-12. Compare Solomon's long days in I Kings 3:14 with the Messiah's here and in Acts 2:24. The grave couldn't hold Him; Death couldn't keep Him; Hell couldn't stand Him; And heaven couldn't wait for Him!

Third, "The pleasure (purpose, will) of the LORD shall prosper in or through His hand." How? Well, for one! He fulfilled the whole council of God by willingly offering His soul as a 'Trespass Offering' and that was a big ONE! Then let me give you four more: Through the service of His mediation, I Tim. 2:5; Heb. 7:25; Isa. 53:12; Through the sacrifice of His body & soul which can never be repeated, I Jn. 2:2; Heb. 10:12; Through the sanctification of His bride, the church, Heb. 2:10-11; 10:10; 13:12; I Cor. 6:11; Through the salvation of all mankind, Acts 4:12; John 14:6; Joel 2:32; Ps. 116:12-13. Therefore, He and He alone effects the ultimate success of *YeHoVaH's* program and this success was sealed at Calvary where He cried triumphantly from Calvary (*tetelestai*); **"FINISHED!"**

Isaiah saw it, Daniel saw it, Hosea, Joel, Amos etc, saw it, but the question is; Do you see it? He shall see His seed (*zera*) descendants; He shall prolong *(arak)* draw out, lengthen, defer His days, His days will be unending; And the will of the LORD shall prosper (*salah*) be powerful, be victorious, come forcefully and grant prosperity. When? After He makes His soul (*neph-esh*) breath, life force, seat of His emotions, the immaterial part of His person, a Sin-Offering, an (*a-sham*) a trespass offering and not before.

Another promise from *YeHoVaH*: **One** - "Not a bone will be broken." Ex. 12:46; Num. 9:12; Ps. 34:20; Jn. 19:36; **Two** – "He would not leave His soul in *sheol* or let His body see corruption (*sahat*-decay);" Psalm 16:10. **WOW!!** (The implications of this are amazing!) He was put in a rich man's cold, stone tomb on Friday evening just before sundown and the Sabbath began, and arose very early in the morning just before sunrise on Sunday morning. Thus fulfilling the culture and custom of Judaism that any part of a day or night is considered a day and a night (Alfred Edersheim). Also Scripture is clear that He would rise **'on'** the third day not **'after'** the third day. Luke 24:21; Mk. 16:9.

The resurrection of Israel's Messiah is the Keystone, the Capstone, and the Cornerstone of their faith and the bottom line of Christianity. Prove it wrong and Christianity sinks like the Titanic. However, I must warn you, it still remains the greatest attested fact of history in the world today! In fact it is the apex, the vertex, the summit, the pinnacle, the zenith, which holds Christianity above every other religion in the world.

Jesus Christ of Nazareth is the only major world religious leader whoever claimed to be God and the only one who physically arose from the dead and ascended into heaven and it was witnessed by over 500 people at once. There's still enough empirical evidence to prove it beyond a reasonable shadow of a doubt today. In fact any person, who sets out to prove the resurrection of Jesus Christ is false, with an open mind, will become a believer in the resurrection and in Jesus Christ and if they are truly honest with themselves and God, will become a follower of Jesus Christ! Paul said in, I Cor. 15:12-19, "Without it the resurrection, we are of all men, most miserable." The resurrection of Christ is the 'Bottom Line' of all you hold dear; of all you believe in, in fact it is the foundation your faith is built upon!

****

Part Two: The Servant's Soul Satisfies – Isa. 53:11

The Servant's Soul Satisfies, gratifies, fulfills, fills to repletion, to overflowing, to super abounding. To use a New testament word for it, "Redound" fits, II Cor. 4:15, exceedingly, abundantly, above and beyond, super abounding, super satisfying!!! **"The Servant's Soul Super-Satisfies!!" Now,** the likeness between these three translations is amazing.

> "The Lord also is pleased to take away from the travail of his soul, **to show him light**, and to form him with understanding; to justify the just one who serves many well; and he shall bear their sins." **Septuagint Lxx,** Trans. 1978.

> "Of the travail of his soul he shall see to the full, even My servant, Who by his knowledge did justify the <u>Righteous One</u> to the many, And their iniquities he did bear." **JPS** Trans. 1975.

> "He shall see of the travail of his soul, and shall be satisfied; by his knowledge shall my righteous servant justify many; for he shall bear their iniquities." **KJV** Trans. 1967.

"He shall see of the travail of His 'soul' and shall be satisfied;" In v. 10 the Resurrection of the Servant/Messiah was in view, but in v. 11 the Justification of the Servant/Messiah is in view and God's Justification is only applied to those who have a personal knowledge and a personal relationship with the Servant/Messiah. "He shall see the travail (*amal* - toilsome labor, misery, sorrow, grievance, Birth-Pangs) of his **soul** (*nephesh*) and shall be satisfied;" However, this word is not usually associated with labor pains but with iniquity and has the negative connotations of wretchedness as in, Isa. 59:4.

This Servant will inherit the right to rule His kingdom, Isa. 53:12; Ps. 2:6-8; Ps. 110; Rev. 19:11-16: Why? Because He willingly poured out His **soul** (*nephesh*) unto death; Because, He was humble enough to be numbered with transgressors; Because, He was willing to bare the sin of many, namely the world, the (*kosmos*); Because, He is continually making intercession on behalf of others right now. All this after the Servant is crushed, bruised, beaten and pierced through.

Isaiah is looking back on v. 1-10, on those graphic words he wrote; rejected, despised, stricken, smitten, wounded, chastised, stripped, oppressed, afflicted, slaughtered, cut-off, deaths, trespass offering, alone, marred, deformed, grief. This Servant, Israel's Messiah travailed (*amal*) in His soul that billions and billions might be born of the Word and of the Spirit to His eternal joy and ours, Heb. 12:2, "Who for the joy that was set before Him, endured the cross, despising the shame, and is set down at the right hand of the throne of God!" WOW! Can you fathome that? Can you really comprehend its value and worth?

Listen to the next two verses, Heb. 12:3-4, "For consider (contemplate, estimate) Him that endured such contradiction of sinners against Himself, lest you be wearied and faint in your minds. You have not yet resisted unto blood, striving against sin." (What did He mean by that?)

The whole scope of the **'Cup'** and its dregs are in view here, 'The Whole Cup!' His words come to mind here, in the garden, "O My Father, if it be possible let this **cup** pass from Me; <u>**nevertheless**</u>, not as I will, but as Thou wilt." Matt. 26:39. (That is one of the most powerful words you can master to defeat the enemy, "Nevertheless!" It is used almost 100 times in the Scriptures and almost 13 different Hebrew and Greek words are used to translate it. Books have been written on the word, 'Nevertheless!'

Again we are reminded of Matt. 26:38, the verse just before this one, "My **soul** (*psuche*) is exceedingly sorrowful (*peril-oo-pos*), even unto death; " No wonder He sweat great drops of blood! (*hematohidrosis*). The Soul – is life, heart, mind, breath, the immaterial and eternal part of the inner person, the animate living self, the real you, the seat of your emotions, feelings, desires and affections. That is where love comes from. The soul is the image of God but it is fallow!

He, *YeHoVaH*, the LORD GOD saw it and was satisfied (*saba*). Man may not be satisfied with the blood atonement, but GOD is! Satan may not be convinced of it's completeness otherwise he would stop accusing believers before the Father day and night, Rev. 12:10; but God is! Listen, if the Servant/Messiah must continually plead the merit of His own shed blood, then how much more should we need to rest upon it, accept it and preach it for a sanctified life! Rev. 12:11 says, "And they overcame him (Satan) by the blood of the Lamb, and by the word of His testimony; and they loved not their lives unto death."

Can I ask you a question? Are you satisfied with the Messiah's blood atonement? Are you? Or are you still working out your own salvation? This was *YeHoVaH's* perfect sacrifice; A Propitiation! A Super-Satisfying Sacrifice! God was finally, totally satisfied! The Hebrew word for satisfied is (*saba*) It's like an onomatopoeia, a word spelled like the sound it makes, '*Saba,* Ahhhh!' Not just satisfied, but to have one's full desire super-satisfied, to have excess satisfaction, to be satiated.

The Servant/Messiah would experience an intense satisfaction at the prospect of the new name He would acquire, Savior! The salvation of mankind is on such a scale as to give complete and perfect satisfaction to God the Father, Satisfied! The Holy Spirit is completely satisfied with His new position as Comforter, Teacher, Indweller, and Pointer to Jesus Christ!

Very few of us can say that word and really mean it this side of heaven (*saba!*) especially the self-centered. How do we know *YeHoVaH* was satisfied? The veil was rent from top to bottom giving man direct, immediate, access into God's very presence! Even the rocks were rent; the saints were sent forth into the holy city to bear testimony, in fact the whole earth did quake! Matt. 27:50-54. Then the Spirit was sent Acts 2:23, when He sat down on the right hand of the Father on high on *Shavuot or Pentecost*! (*"Saba - Ahhhh!)* Proving He was who he said He was!

"By His knowledge shall My Righteous Servant justify many;" This is a bold, shocking statement to make. That this man, this Servant, will make people righteous because of what he has done! In fact, 'My Righteous

Servant' is very emphatic in the Hebrew here to express the absolute righteousness of God's Servant, (*Tsadik Ehbed*). The Lawful, Just, Perfect, Servant of the LORD; Remember, Isa. 52:13? "He shall be exalted, extolled, and elevated." Well here He is again, as the, 'Absolute Righteous Servant!'

To 'Justify the many' means to, vindicate or declare them righteous! (Free from guilt and sin!) There is included in this plan, "The Whosoever Will," I Pet. 3:18; John 3:16; Rom. 10:13. In Hebrew, it means to save, but how? By the sprinkling (*nazah*) of His blood, Isa. 52:15. Whatever else you see in this verse, you must see Justification, which is being made right with God! (Comp. Rom. 4:24-25 & II Cor. 5:21 of the N.T. = 'Right Standing With God!). He died for our sin and salvation, but He arose for our Justification; This is the 'Great Transaction' of the Bible! He took our sin and we took His righteousness, in a sense we exchanged garments, our filthy rags for His robe of righteousness.

By His perfect **knowledge** (Whose knowledge? The Servant/Messiah's!) and His understanding of *YeHoVaH's* plan of redemption and His own role in it. He voluntarily went to Calvary and died on the Tree, becoming a curse for us! Gal.3:13. So, in this sense obedience on His part, 'Justifies the many, namely us.' Rom. 5:19; Phil. 2:8. Now, to be Justified, (*Tsadak*) means to be righteous, to be innocent, to be vindicated, in accordance with God's standard implying innocence and His standard is a blood sacrifice, Lev. 17:11.

Several scholars believe that the phrase, "By His knowledge..." refers to, knowledge of Him, the Servant/Messiah. With the idea of becoming fully acquainted with Him and His plan of salvation. (Subjective Knowledge). The Paleo Hebrew word for knowledge is made up of two letters (*dalet*) for door and (*ayin*) for eye; or to see beyond the door, or to see on the other side of the door. The word knowledge is evidently used in a larger sense to denote all that constitutes acquaintance with Him. Phil. 3:10, "That I may know Him, (*ginosko* – experiential knowledge) and the power of His resurrection, and the fellowship of His sufferings..." It is by knowing the Redeemer personally that men are saved. The Servant/Messiah does not save sinners by their enlightenment of Him but by His atoning sacrifice for them. Yet none are saved who do not know Him as their personal Savior by faith alone.

It is only by the knowledge of the Servant/Messiah and by an acquaintance of His character, doctrines, sufferings, death and resurrection that anyone can be justified. John 17:3 says, "And this is life eternal, that they might know Thee the only true God, and Jesus Christ whom Thou hast sent." We have to become acquainted with Him and His doctrines or we can never be regarded or treated as righteous in the sight of a holy God. Now how did He accomplish this?

"For He shall bear their iniquities." Again Isaiah the prophet gives us the very basis by which the Servant/Messiah alone can make many righteous. The word bear is the word (s*abal*) to bear a heavy load or burden, to drag something along. Oh, how heavy our sin is! Their iniquities (*aw-von*) not His own, ours, yours and mine! He had to drag our stinking sin to the Tree at Calvary and nail it there! Col. 2:14. In fact in Hebrew (*pesha*) is crossing the line, rebellion; (*chet*) is missing the mark, omission; (*aw-von*) iniquities is perverted, depraved, crookedness. It comes from the word (*avah*) to bend, twist or distort. Now all three are in view here and used in this context.

How does He bare our sin? By being our Sin-Bearer; Our Savior; Our Redeemer, Joel 2:32, "And it shall come to pass that whosoever shall call on the name of the LORD shall be delivered (*malat - saved*);" And by removing the 'Sin-Barrier' that has separated us from God, Isa. 59:1-2'. He is both Just and Justifier, Rom. 3:26, "To declare, I say, at this time his righteousness, that he might be **just** and the **justifier** of him who believeth in *Yeshua/Jesus*." The most mysterious and yet the most glorious thing about the death of *Yeshua/Jesus* is that He was God's sacrificial Lamb! In the same way, in which we cannot begin to comprehend, He took our place on the Tree, bearing the righteous judgment of God against our sin. We know so little of this sacrifice.

It was not merely submission; it was direct, positive, consecration of His entire being and soul! He placed Himself on the altar and then became Himself the sacrificing High Priest! This was not some martyr, or frustrated Jew dying for some cause, this was the 'Lamb of God' John 1:29, dying for all mankind, the fulfillment of Gen. 22:8, "My son, God will provide Himself *(as)* a lamb for a burnt offering: so they went both of them together." But He provided a ram (*ah-yil*) not a lamb (*sey*) that day and the word **Himself** is a reflexive pronoun pointing back to God. John 8:56,

"Abraham rejoiced to see My day and he saw it and was glad!" When did he see it? On Mt. Moriah, with his son Isaac, in the Angel of the LORD. On the same note, Justification is only applied to those who have a personal knowledge and a personal relationship with God's Servant, only those who have experienced the, 'New Birth!'

This last phrase in v. 11, like the first one goes beyond the Servant/Messiah's finished work and points to His continuous work of mediation. Heb. 7:25; 8:6; Isa. 53:12. We are not declared righteous like it was magic and He had some mystic, magical powers but He, "...bore our sins, in His own body on the tree, that we being dead to sins, should live unto righteousness; by whose stripes you were healed." I Peter 2:24. He bore our sins in His own body on the Tree, can you fathom that? Can you even begin to comprehend the immensity of that concept?

A holy, perfect, incarnate God, bore your sin so you could be justified, not just forgiven and forgotten for all your filthy rags Isa. 64:6, but paid for in full, to the last farthing! "For Christ also has once suffered for sins, the just for the unjust, that He might bring us to God, being put to death in the flesh but made alive by the Spirit;" I Peter 3:18. As Jesus said to Nicodemus, a Pharisee, a member of the Sanhedrin and 'The Teacher of Israel,' "Except a man be born again (*anothen* - born from above) he cannot see, he never will see the kingdom of God." Jn. 3:3.

****

Part Three: The Servant's Soul Supplicates – Isa. 53:12

To petition is usually asking for yourself, intercession is asking for others, but a supplication is asking with tears. Supplication is to ask humbly and earnestly, to entreat, beseech, implore, adjure, importune, beg. Webster likes to express the meaning of supplication with these very synonyms. To 'Beg' suggests, earnestness or insistence, especially in asking for a favor; To 'Entreat' implies, an effort to persuade or to overcome resistance; To 'Beseech' implies, great earnestness or anxiety, "I beseech you to have mercy!" to 'Implore' adds to 'Beseech' a suggestion of greater urgency

"Therefore he shall inherit many, and he shall divide the spoils of the mighty; because his soul was delivered to death: and he was numbered among the transgressors; and he bore the sins of many, and was delivered because of their iniquities." **LXX, Trans. 1978**

"Therefore will I divide him a portion among the great, And he shall divide the spoil with the mighty; Because he bared his soul unto death, And was numbered with the transgressors; Yet he bore the sin of many, And made intercession for the transgressors." **JPS, Trans. 1975**

"Therefore will I divide him a portion with the great, and he shall divide the spoil with the strong, because he has poured out his soul unto death; and he was numbered with the transgressors; and he bore the sin of many, and made intercession for the for the transgressors." **KJV, Trans. 1967**

In v.10 we saw the Servant/Messiah's Resurrection; *'After'* his **soul** became an (*asham*) a trespass-offering; He saw his seed, His days were prolonged, and the pleasure of the LORD prospered in His hand. In v.11 we saw the Servant/Messiah's Justification; *'After'* the travail (*amal*) labor, misery, sorrow, birth-pangs of His **soul**, He justified the many; However, here in v.12 we see the Servant/Messiah's Imputation, *'After'* His **soul** is delivered unto death! In v.12 we get a glimpse of the Servant/Messiah's future kingdom as well as His 'Second Coming!' If there is any doubt left in your mind after v. 1-11 how this Servant/Messiah could bring God's justice into this hell bound world, this verse should answer your questions! (By the way, if this Servant/Messiah is not Jesus Christ of Nazareth, then Jesus did an incredible job of impersonating this Servant!)

"Therefore 'will I' divide Him a portion with the great and 'He shall' divide the spoil with the strong," (I YeHoVaH will divide it to Him – and immediately following – He the Messiah shall divide it. So Christ completed His work and God completed His promise to Him for it!) The LORD *YeHoVaH* will give Him the mighty, the great ones (*barabbim*) and the many, the strong ones (*asum*) mighty, powerful ones for a portion and the Servant/Messiah shall divide the spoils. The spoil which God divides to the Servant/Messiah, He divides among His followers; It's the exact same word; For when He led captivity captive, He gave gifts unto men. Eph. 4:8; Ps. 68:18; Acts 20:35; Luke 14:12 This Messiah conquered for us and through Him we are more than conquerors. Rom. 8:37.

Why, well the battle is over, and it's time to divide the spoils and the Servant/Messiah deserves a 'Lion's Share' to say the least and the LORD tells us why He deserves such a large portion. The word 'portion' is added for clarification, it is not in the Hebrew text, that's why the LXX leaves it out; "Therefore he shall inherit many, and he shall divide the spoils of the mighty;" Dr. Whitcomb says, "The great ones and strong ones are the saints of all ages." (Some interpret this as Satan). They will surround Him and fight with Him in the day of His power; Ps. 2; 72; 110:5; Rev. 19:14. This truth is more about Israel than the Church, Mal. 4:3; Ps. 110:1-3.

However, we do see I Peter 1:11 and its theme expounded once again, "Searching what, or what manner of time the Spirit of Christ who was in them did signify, when He testified beforehand the sufferings of Christ and the glory that should follow." (Glory always follows suffering!) "For I reckon that the sufferings of this present time are not worthy to be compared with the glory which shall be revealed in us." Rom. 8:18. Whatever you do with v.12, it has been claimed that no verse in the Older Testament presents more problems than this one, and yet it is obvious that a note of triumph prevails throughout it. The speaker is God, and the Servant/Messiah is the primary agent who divides the spoils of the victory with the mighty. The many and the strong are the spiritual seed mentioned in v.10; His people participate in the enjoyment of the spoils of His victory. Now, why is *YeHoVaH* going to do all this for His Servant/Messiah? The rest of the verse answers that in four clauses:

First - "Because He has poured out His soul unto death;" The word poured (*arah*) means to uncover, to empty, to make bare naked, nude, to leave destitute, to lay bare by emptying. The JPS translation has, "Because he bared his soul unto death." Life resides in the blood and when the blood is poured out, life flows out with it. If all your blood leaves your body, you die! "Because he poured out His soul (*nephesh* - life, breathe) unto death;" Heb. 9:22, In the law, blood is always connected with forgiveness, especially the 'shedding' of blood. John 19:34.

Lev. 17:11 says, "For the life of the flesh is in the blood; and I have given it to you upon the altar to make atonement for your souls; for it is the blood that makes an atonement for the soul." Rom. 3:25 says, "Whom God has set forth to be a propitiation (satisfying sacrifice, a *saba*) through faith in His blood (*Mashiach's*), to declare His righteousness for the remission of sins that are past, through the forbearance of God;" He voluntarily did this on His own, no man took His life, they couldn't, it was impossible! How could any finite man, kill an infinite God? (IMPOSSIBLE!)

If He was the infinite God-Man, He had to willingly lay it down, just like he said in John 10:17-18, "Therefore does My Father love Me because I lay down My life, that I might take it again. No Man takes it from Me, but I lay it down of Myself. I have the power to lay it down and I have the power to take it again. This commandment have I received of My Father." The word death (*lammaveth*) in Isa. 53:12, is an intensive plural for deaths once again, refer back to v.9 for a further explanation. In fact 13 times in this passage it is mentioned that this Servant/Messiah bore the suffering for others. That seems to be the central theme in this passage and His mission. In the Newer Testament the central theme is the Cross!

Second - "And He was numbered with the transgressors;" He was numbered (*mana*) counted, reckoned, assigned, appointed, with the transgressors (*pesha*) wicked, evil, violent, rebellious criminals. These were not just sinners, they were malefactors Luke 12:32, evil doers, wicked, evil, destructive, 'Bad Dudes!' This verb is reflexive so He permitted Himself to be numbered with them. He was considered a transgressor by those who sat in judgment of Him and sentenced Him to die and to be buried in the Valley of *Hinnom* with the criminals; actually their bodies were just thrown on the garbage dump, for the animals to devour.

However, he was accused of blasphemy and for that crime He was to be buried in a grave, in the valley of *Hinnom,* polluted with pig's blood, with His cross member, to bear His shame for ever. First, He was to be crucified between two criminals because the one in the center was guilty of the most heinous of all crimes, but as per the JPS translation of v.9, "They made or assigned his grave with the wicked and his tomb with the rich;" (How ironic is that!) This prophecy was fulfilled perfectly as He was buried in a rich man's, hand carved tomb and wrapped in an expensive linen cloth, soaked with 100 pounds of myrrh and aloes, valued at around, $50,000.00. He did not merely die **with** the malefactors; he died **for** them and that makes all the difference in the world! He didn't die for His sin and rebellion but for yours!

Third - "And He bore the sin of many;" He bore (*nasa*) to lift, to bear up, to carry away, or to take away; (I like that!) It is used 18x of an armor-bearer and it's also translated, 'to forgive!' (Very Interesting!) "He forgave the sin of many." Only God can forgive sin, man can forgive a debt, he can even forgive a wrong done to him, but he cannot forgive sin against God's laws or standards! Even a Supreme Court justice can't do that!

However, the Servant/Messiah could do that, so He must have been more than man, He must have been the infinite God-Man! This word is very different from v.11, "He shall bear (*sabal*) their iniquities;" There the word meant to drag along like a heavy load, to the Tree on Calvary and nail it there. Here the word means to lift it up, bear it up, take it away, not cover it up but wash them away forever! Interesting as I mentioned before, our word today, "NASA," stands for 'National Aeronautics Space Administration' or lifting up rockets, space stations and satellites into the sky. I wonder if they used this same acronym? Here we see substitutionary, vicarious atonement and forgiveness, a whole new concept, to the Jewish mind!

To take away our sin forever, not cover it up (*kafar*) not atone for it, or pacify it but 'Eradicate It' once and for all, forever! This is (*chet*) missing the mark, an action contrary to the will and law of God, with a strong implication of guilt that follows. This Servant paid a debt He didn't owe because we owed a debt we couldn't pay, simple as that! The verbs relating to this vicarious sacrifice are in the perfect tense, describing a completed action.

However, the verb referring to intercession is in the imperfect tense, describing incomplete action, something that continues on. Therefore, this Servant/Messiah meets man's two greatest needs: the need for a Savior and the need for a High Priest.

Fourth - "And made intercession for the transgressors." He made intercession (*paga*) this word means to encounter, meet, reach, join, to reach the mark; It is written in the imperfect tense, meaning continuous action! This verb means to go all out on behalf of another person, to go the extra mile, to give him your cloak and your coat; Don't just give him the shirt off your back throw in your shoes too! He bore the sin (*chet*) of many, 'to miss the mark,' and here the Servant/Messiah makes (*paga*) intercession to 'reach the mark' for the transgressors (*pesha*) the rebels and revilers. We miss the mark and He hits the mark, every time! This is the present work of the Servant/Messiah right now I John 2:1; Heb. 7:25; 8:6; Isa. 53:12.

However, the Servant is not just the Savior of the Scriptures, He is the Sin-Bearer of the Nations too, Isa. 52:15. Not just Israel, but the *Goi'im*, the nations as well, and He is making intercession for all right now, Heb. 10:10-12; 7:25; Rev. 12:11. There is a lot more going on here with this Servant/Messiah than just words regarding His high priestly intercession. He is pleading the merit and virtue of His atoning work as the only ground of acceptance for the transgressors for whom He died.

The basis for the intercession is the substitutionary expiation of the Servant/Messiah, who poured out His life's blood on a Tree on Calvary to pay the penalty in full for man's sin. This intercession refers not merely to prayer but includes the bearing away (*nasa*) of our sin. As the Redeemer, our High Priest presents the merit of His atoning blood before the 'Throne of Mercy' and pleads for the souls of men.

Rev. 5:12 says, "Worthy is the Lamb that was slain to receive power, and riches, and wisdom, and strength, and honor, and glory, and blessing." Far from being a transgressor this Servant/Messiah was the Savior of transgressors and interceded for them at the very moment they were putting Him to death on the Tree! Luke 23:34, And cried, "Father forgive them for they know not what they do!"

Some feel the intercession was more of an intervention where He took the sinners place in suffering and death. <u>The problem with that is the imperfect tense verb for interceding; He is not continually dying to atone for our sins but He is continually interceding on our behalf. For the many whose guilt He bore that they might understand what He has done and accept the justification He achieved when He bore their sins on the Tree in v.11.</u>

Franz Delitzsch stated, "The Servant of Jehovah goes through shame to glory and through death to life. He conquers when He yields; He rules after being enslaved; He lives after He has died; He completes His work after He Himself has been apparently cut-off. His glory streams upon the dark ground of the deepest humiliation..." We can only say that apart from *Yeshua ha Mashiach*, Jesus the Christ, it would be impossible to understand this 'Crown Jewel' in Isaiah and it would forever be a dark mystery with no solution.

However, in the light of His life it has become the brightest jewel in Hebrew prophecy, the star of hope and the salvation of all mankind. The 'Suffering Servant' is revealed in 'His High Priestly' ministry in v.12, "He bore the sin of many." He became our Sin-Bearer, I Pet. 2:24; Our intercessor, Heb. 7:25; Our mediator, I Tim. 2:5; And our 'Sin Offering,' II Cor. 5:21. All this led Him to the Tree on Calvary; does it lead you to the Tree? <u>The Tree is not only an object we come to for salvation from God, it is an object we cling to for service for God</u>!

C.H. Spurgeon said, "It was as if Hell were placed in His cup and He seized it with both hands, lifted it up to His father, thanked Him for it and with one mighty draught of love, drank damnation dry." This Servant took your Hell, that you might take His heaven, think about that.... All this Jesus Christ has done for you, what have you ever done for Him?

King David was rejected and sent into exile due to Israel being in rebellion against God. He sent this message to the elders of Judah, *Yeshua/Jesus* sends the same message to Israel today and to every Jewish person and to us: "You are my brethren, you are my bones and my flesh. Why then are you the last to bring back the King?" II Sam. 19:12. ***"WHY?"*** "Behold My Servant!".......... Israel or Messiah? You Choose! And you must choose! Because no decision is in fact, "A Decision of Rejection!" But choose wisely and choose decisively and choose today, tomorrow may be to late!!!

PRAYER - "Abba, Father, help us to choose and to choose wisely, because this choice will decide where we spend eternity. We all have eternal life, that is a fact, where we spend it is a gift from You. So please, help us to choose wisely and to do it soon before it is too late. *In ha shem Yeshua we pray, Amen!*"

Ancient Rabbinic Sayings-

'Rabbinic Thoughts on Isaiah 53'

1. The Targum of Jonathan ben Uziel (2nd century) reprinted by Oxford at the Clarendon Press, 1953 titled, "The Targum of Isaiah" renders Isaiah 52:13 this way: *"Behold, my servant, the Messiah, shall prosper; He shall be exalted, and increase and be very strong."*

2. The Babylonian Talmud, Sanhedrin 98v (codified in the 6th century) says this of Isaiah 53: *"The Messiah — what is His name? ... The Rabbis say, 'The leprous one;' those of the house of the Rabbi say, 'The sick one,' as it is said, 'surely he hath borne our sickness.'"*

3. Rabbi Moses Maimonides, 'Rambam:' *"Whoever does not believe in him (Messiah), or does not await his coming, denies not only the other prophets but also the Torah and Moses, our teacher, for the Torah attests to his coming."* Source: Hilchos Melachim from the Mishneh Torah of Rambam, 11:1.

4. Rabbi Mosheh el Sheikh, commonly known as Alshech, chief Rabbi of Safed in the (16th century) in his 'Commentaries on the Earlier Prophets' wrote on Isaiah 53: *"I may remark, then, that our rabbis with one voice accept and affirm the opinion that the prophet is speaking of the King Messiah, and we ourselves also adhere to the same view."*

5. The Zohar, the principal work of the Kabbala, a thirteenth century commentary on mystical elements of the Bible, on Isaiah 53: *'When Israel was in the Holy Land, they had their sufferings and afflictions removed from them by their prayers and sacrifices; but now the Messiah removes them from the children of the world. – When the Holy One, blessed be He, wishes the recovery of the children of the world, He afflicts one righteous person from their midst, and for His sake all are healed. How is this known? It is written, 'He was wounded for our transgressions, He was bruised for our iniquities... and with his stripes we are healed' (Isaiah 53:5). (Part II, fol. 212a and Part III, fol. 218a, Amsterdam edition)*

6. Midrash (Talmudic commentary) to Ruth 2:14 and Isaiah 53: *'And dip thy morsel in the vinegar' refers to the sufferings (of the Messiah) as it is said: 'But he was wounded because of our transgressions' (Isaiah 53:5).*

7. Sanhedrin (98b), a tractate from the Talmud, commenting on Isaiah 53: *"Messiah... what is His name?"* The disciples of the School of the Rabbi (Jehudah Ha-nassi, the author of the Mishnah) said: Cholaja (The sickly), for it says (Isaiah 53:4): *'Surely he hath born our sicknesses and carried our pains; and we did regard him stricken, smitten of God and afflicted'.*

8. Pesikta Rabbati, a ninth century collection of sermons on Bible topics; on Isaiah 61:10 and Isaiah 53: *'The world-fathers (the patriarchs) will one day in the month of Nisan arise and say to (the Messiah): "Ephraim our righteous Anointed, although we are Thy grandparents yet Thou art greater then we, for Thou hast borne the sins of our children"*, as it says (Isaiah 53:4-5): *'But surely he hath borne our sicknesses and carried our pains; yet we did esteem him stricken, smitten of God and afflicted. But he was pierced because of our transgression, he was bruised for our iniquities: the chastisement of our peace was laid upon him and through his wounds we are healed'. "Great oppressions were laid upon Thee"*, as it says (Isaiah 53:8): *'By oppression and judgement he was taken away; but who considered in his time, that he was cut off out of the land of the living, that he was stricken because of the sins of our children'*, as it says (Isaiah 53:6): *'But the Lord hath laid on him the guilt of us all'.*

9. Luchoth Habberith, Talmudic tractate (242a); *'He (the Messiah) will give Himself and His life over unto death, and His blood will atone for His people.'*

10. Sebanim, (6a) also from the Talmud says: *'Surely atonement can only be made with the blood, as it says, 'For it is the blood that makes atonement by reason of the life.'* Leviticus 17:11 (See also Yoma (5a); and Hebrews 9:22).

11. Sukkah (52a) from the Talmud and Rashi an 11th century French Rabbi state on Zechariah 12:10: *'It is well according to him who explains that the cause (of the mourning) is the slaying of the Messiah, the son of Joseph, since that well agrees with the scripture verse:' "And they shall look upon me, whom they have pierced; and shall mourn for him; as one mourneth for*

his only son." – Rashi. Our Rabbis interpreted it as referring to Messiah ben Joseph.

12. Rabbi Mosheh el Sheikh, known as Alshech, Chief Rabbi of Safed in the 16th Cen. wrote: *'They shall look unto me,'* for they shall lift up their eyes unto Me in perfect repentance, *'when they see Him whom they have pierced,'* that is Messiah, the Son of Joseph; for our Rabbis, of blessed memory, have said that He will take upon Himself all the guilt of Israel, and shall then be slain in the war to make atonement; in such manner that it shall be accounted as if Israel had pierced Him, for on account of their sin He has died; and, therefore, in order that it may be reckoned to them as a perfect atonement, they will repent and look to the blessed One, saying that there is none beside Him, to forgive those that mourn, on account of Him who died for their sin: this is the meaning of, *"They shall look upon Me."*

13. Rabbi Elijah de Vidas a 16th Cen. Rabbi of Safed stated; *'Since the Messiah bears our iniquities…it follows that whoso will not admit that the Messiah thus suffers for our iniquities, must endure and suffer them himself.'*

14. The Zohar, the "Bible" of Jewish mysticism compiled around 110 c.e. applies Isa. 53:4 specifically to the suffering of a sin-bearing Messiah: *"There is in the Garden of Eden a palace called The Palace of the Sons of Sickness; this palace the Messiah then enters, and summons every sickness, every pain, and every chastisement of Israel; they all come and rest upon Him. And were it not that he had thus lighted them off Israel and taken them upon Himself, there had been no man able to bear Israel's chastisement for transgression of the law; and this is that which is written, 'Surely our sickness he had carried…,"*

15. An interesting passage from the *Machzor*, a prayer book for the 'Day of Atonement' written in the 8th century c.e. by Rabbi Eliezer Ha-Kallir, which is not found in the modern versions, but reflects the cry of a people who fear their sin-bearing Messiah may have come for them some time in the past and they failed to recognize Him or worse, they may have rejected Him! *"We are shrunk up in our misery even until now! Our rock hath not come nigh to us: Messiah, our righteousness, hath turned from us; we are in terror, and there is none to justify us! Our iniquities and the yoke of our transgressions he will bear,* **for he was wounded for our transgressions**:

*he will carry our sins upon his shoulder, that we may find forgiveness for our iniquities, and **by his stripes we are healed**. O eternal One, the time is come to make a new creation: from the vault of heaven bring him up, out of Seir draw him forth, that he may make his voice heard to us in Lebanon, a second time by the hand of Yinnon!"* (A Rabbinical name of Messiah derived from Psalm 72:17)

16. Another **'Musaf Service Prayer'** for the **'Day of Atonement'** (David Levy, Prayers for the Day of Atonement, 2nd edition, London, 1807, vol. III, Pg. 37) reads; *"Messiah our Righteousness has departed from us. We shudder; for there is none to justify us. He bears our load of transgression and the burden of our guilt on His shoulder, to effect forgiveness of our sins. He bled for our salvation. O, Eternal One, the time has come that Thou shouldest create Him anew! O bring Him up from the terrestrial sphere. Raise Him up from the land of Seir, to assemble us on Mt. Lebanon, a second time, by the power of Yinnon!"* (A Rabbinical name of Messiah derived from Psalm 72:17)

17. Gershom Scholem in "Sabbatai Sevi" pg. 53-54, says, *"In the Tannaitic period (Repeaters/Teachers of the Oral Law, 10-220 CE) the 'suffering servant' passages had occasionally been interpreted as referring to the Messiah, but later Haggadicts as well as medieval commentators preferred different interpretations. In order to undermine Christian exegesis, he was interpreted as a figure of Moses, or of Israel, or of the pious in general. In Jewish/Christian disputations the Jewish spokesman always denied that the passages referred to the Messiah."*

18. Rabbi Joseph ben Kaspi, 1280-1340 CE warned the Rabbis that *"Those who expounded this section of the Messiah give occasion to the heretics (Christians) to interpret it of Jesus."* In response to this rabbi Saadia ibn Danan said, *"May God forgive him for not having spoken the truth."* (S. R. Driver & Adolf Nebauer, "The Suffering Servant of Isaiah According to Jewish Tradition," pg. 203.

19. Rabbi Naphtali ben Asher Altschuler 16th & 17th centuries stated; *"I am surprised that Rashi and David Kimchi have not, with the Targum, also applied them (vv. 52:13 – 53:12) to the Messiah."* S. R. Driver & Adolf Nebauer, The Suffering Servant of Isaiah According to Jewish Tradition," pg. 319.

20. Rabbi Moses Maimonides: *"What is the manner of Messiah's advent....there shall rise up one of whom none have known before, and signs and wonders which they shall see performed by him will be the proofs of his true origin; for the Almighty, where he declares to us his mind upon this matter, says, 'Behold a man whose name is the Branch, and he shall branch forth out of his place' (Zech. 6:12). And Isaiah speaks similarly of the time when he shall appear, without father or mother or family being known, He came up as a sucker before him, and as a root out of dry earth, etc....in the words of Isaiah, when describing the manner in which kings will harken to him, At him kings will shut their mouth; for that which had not been told them have they seen, and that which they had not heard they have perceived."* (From the Letter to the South (*Yemen*), quoted in The Fifty-third Chapter of Isaiah According to the Jewish Interpreters, *Ktav* Publishing House, 1969, Volume 2, pages 374-5).

21. *Pesikta*, cited in the treatise *Abkath Rokhel*, and reprinted in *Hulsii* Theologia Judaica, where this passage occurs, p. 309: *"When Elohim created the world, He stretched out His hand under the throne of His kavod, and brought forth the being of the Messiah. He said to him: 'Will you heal and redeem My sons after 6000 years?' He answered him, 'I will. 'Then Elohim said to him: 'Will you then also bear the punishment in order to blot out their sins, as it is written, "But he bore our diseases" (Yesha'yahu 53:4). And the Messiah answered Him; 'I will joyfully bear them'* (cf. *Zohar*, 2:212a).

22. Rabbi Moshe Kohen ibn Crispin, of Cordova and afterwards Toledo (14th Century) in Spain, says: *"Those who for controversial reasons apply the prophecy of the suffering servant to Israel find it impossible to understand the true meaning of this prophecy, having forsaken the knowledge of our teachers, and inclined after the stubbornness of their own opinions. Their misinterpretation distorts the passage from its natural meaning, for it was given of God as a description of the Messiah, whereby, when any should claim to be the Messiah, to judge by the resemblance or non-resemblance to it whether he were the Messiah or not."*

Rabbi Crispin also said: *"I am pleased to interpret the passage in accordance with the teaching of our Rabbis of the King Messiah...and adhere to the literal sense. Thus shall I be free from forced and far-fetched interpretations of which others are guilty."*

Rabbi Crispin also said: *"This prophecy was delivered by Isaiah at the divine command for the purpose of making known to us something about the nature of the future Messiah, who is to come and deliver Israel...in order that if any should arise claiming to be himself the Messiah, we may reflect and look to see whether we can observe in him any resemblance to the traits described here: if there is a resemblance, than we may believe that he is the Messiah our Righteous; but if not, we cannot do so."* S. R. Driver & Adolf Nebauer, The Suffering Servant of Isaiah According to Jewish Tradition, p. 114, 199ff.

23. Rabbi Moses Haddersham states, "Immediately the Messiah, out of love, took upon himself all those plagues and sufferings, as it is written in Yeshayahu 53; 'He was abused and oppressed!'

24. Yefeth ben Ali stated, "And the Lord laid on him the iniquity of us all." The prophet does not by (*avon*) mean iniquity, but punishment for iniquity, as in the passage, "Be sure your sin will find you out." Num. 32:23; Driver & Neubauer, pg. 26; Soloff, pg. 109.

25. Maimonides himself affirmed the messianic interpretation of Isaiah 53 (Patai, vol. 1, pg. 322) "Finally the idea that God would place the sins of Israel upon an innocent man is alluded to in this Midrash: Moses spake before the Holy One, blessed be He, 'Will not a time come upon when Israel will have neither Tabernacle or Temple? What will happen to them (as regards atonement)?" He replied, 'I will take a righteous man from amongst them and make him a pledge on their account, and I will atone for their iniquities.' Midrash on Exodus 35:4.

26. Isaac Abravanel/Abarbanel stated, "Christian scholars interpret Isaiah 53 as referring to 'that man' who was crucified in Jerusalem about the end of the Second Temple and who according to their view was the Son of God who became a man in the womb of a Virgin. Jonathan ben Uziel explains it as the Messiah who has yet to come and this is the opinion of the ancients in many of Midrashim." (So, even the synagogue and its leaders could not help acknowledging that this passage is about their Messiah, predicting His death and glory and it is not referring to Israel.)

****

Endnotes-

THE TEXT

Isaiah 52:13 – 53:12

… as it appears in the Jewish and Gentile Scriptures …

52:13. Behold, My servant shall prosper, He shall be exalted and be lifted up, and shall be very high. **14.** According as many were appalled at thee—So marred was his visage unlike that of a man, And his form unlike that of the sons of men— **15.** So shall he startle many nations, Kings shall shut their mouths because of him; For that which had not been told them shall they see, And that which they had not heard shall they perceive.

53:1. 'Who would have believed our report? And to whom hath the arm of the LORD been revealed? **2.** For he shot up right forth as a sapling, And as a root out of a dry ground; He had no form nor comeliness, that we should look upon him, Nor beauty that we should delight in him. **3.** He was despised, and forsaken of men, A man of pains, and acquainted with disease, And as one from whom men hide their face: He was despised, and we esteemed him not. **4.** Surely our diseases he did bear, and our pains he carried; Whereas we did esteem him stricken, Smitten of God, and afflicted. **5.** But he was wounded because of our transgressions, he was crushed because of our iniquities; The chastisement of our welfare was upon him, And with his stripes we were healed. **6.** All we like sheep did go astray, We turned every one to his own way; And the LORD hath made to light on him The iniquity of us all. **7.** He was oppressed though he humbled himself And opened not his mouth; As a lamb that is led to the slaughter, And as a sheep that before her shearers is dumb; Yea, he opened not his mouth. **8.** By oppression and judgment he was taken away, And with his generation who did reason? For he was cut off out of the land of the living, For the transgression of my people to whom the stroke was due. **9.** And they made his grave with the wicked, And with the rich his tomb; Although he had done no violence, Neither was any deceit in his mouth.' **10.** Yet it pleased the LORD to crush him by disease; To see if his soul would offer itself in restitution, That he might see his seed, prolong his days, And that the purpose of the LORD might prosper by his hand: **11.** Of the travail of his soul he shall see to the full, even My servant, the Righteous One to the many, And their iniquities he did bear. **12.** Therefore will I divide him a portion among the great, And he shall divide the spoil with the mighty; Because he bared his soul unto death, And was numbered with the transgressors; Yet he bore the sin of many, And made intercession for the transgressors.

'Jewish Publication Society'

52:13. Behold, my servant shall deal prudently; he shall be exalted and extolled and be very high. **14.** As many were astounded at thee—his visage was so marred more than any man, and his form more than the sons of men—**15.** So shall he sprinkle many nations; the kings shall shut their mouths at him; for that which had not been told them shall they see, and that which they had not heard shall they consider.

53:1. Who hath believed our report? And to whom is the arm of the LORD revealed? **2.** For he shall grow up before him like a tender plant, and like a root out of a dry ground; he hath no form nor comeliness, and when we shall see him, there is no beauty that we should desire him. **3.** He is despised and rejected of men, a man of sorrows, and acquainted with grief, and we hid as it were our faces from him; he was despised, and we esteemed him not. **4.** Surely he hath borne our griefs, and carried our sorrows; yet we did esteem him stricken, smitten of God, and afflicted. **5.** But he was wounded for our transgressions, he was bruised for our iniquities; the chastisement for our peace was upon him, and with his stripes we are healed. **6.** All we like sheep have gone astray; we have turned every one to his own way, and the LORD hath laid on him the iniquity of us all. **7.** He was oppressed, and he was afflicted, yet he opened not his mouth; he is brought as a lamb to the slaughter, and as a sheep before her shearers is dumb, so he openeth not his mouth. **8.** He was taken from prison and from judgment; and who shall declare his generation? For he was cut off out of the land of the living; for the transgression of my people was he stricken. **9.** And he made his grave with the wicked, and with the rich in his death, because he had done no violence, neither was any deceit in his mouth. **10.** Yet it pleased the LORD to bruise him; he hath put him to grief. When thou shalt make his soul an offering for sin, he shall see his seed, he shall prolong his days, and the pleasure of the LORD shall prosper in his hand. **11.** He shall see of the travail of his soul, and shall be satisfied; by his knowledge shall my righteous servant justify many; for he shall bear their iniquities. **12.** Therefore will I divide him a portion with the great, and he shall divide the spoil with the strong, because he hath poured out his soul unto death; and he was numbered with the transgressors; and he bore the sin of many, and made intercession for the transgressors.

'Kings James Version'

… as it appears in the Greek Septuagint …

"Isaiah 52:13-53:12 – by Sir Lancelot C. L. Brenton 1844"

"Behold, my servant shall understand, and be exalted, and glorified exceedingly. As many shall be amazed at thee, so shall thy face be without glory from men, and thy glory *shall not be honored* by the sons of men. Thus shall many nations wonder/*marvel* at him; and kings shall keep their mouths shut; for they to whom no report was brought concerning him shall see; and they who have not heard, shall consider." Isa. 52:13-15.

"**O Lord**, who has believed our report? And to whom has the arm of the Lord been revealed? We brought a report as of a child before him; he is as a root in a thirsty land: he has no form, nor comeliness; and we saw him, but he had no form nor beauty. But his form was ignoble, and inferior to that of the children of men; he was a man in suffering, and acquainted with the bearing of sickness, for his face is turned from us; he was dishonored and not esteemed. He bears our sins, and is pained for us; yet we accounted him to be in trouble, and in suffering, and in affliction. But he was wounded on account of our sins, and was bruised because of our iniquities: the chastisement of our peace was upon him; and by his bruises we were healed. All we as sheep have gone astray; every one has gone astray in his way; and the Lord gave him up for our sins." Isa. 53:1-6

"And he, because of his affliction, opens not his mouth: he was led as a sheep to the slaughter and as a lamb before the shearer is dumb, so he opens not his mouth. In his humiliation, his judgment was taken away: who shall declare his generation? For his life is taken away from the earth: because of the iniquities of my people he was led to death. And I will give the wicked for his burial, and the rich for his death; for he practiced no iniquity, nor craft with his mouth. The Lord also is pleased to purge him from his stroke. If ye can give an offering for sin, your soul shall see a long-lived seed: the Lord also is pleased to take away from the travail of his soul, **to show him light,** and to form him with understanding; to justify the just one who serves many well; and he shall bear their sins. Therefore, he shall inherit the many, and he shall divide the spoils of the mighty; because his soul was delivered to death; and he was numbered among the transgressors; and he bore the sins of many, and was delivered because of their iniquities." Isa. 53:7-12

"Isaiah 52:13-53:12 – by Charles Thomson 1808"

"Behold, my servant will mind and be exalted and highly glorified. In the same manner as many will be astonished at thee; (so devoid of the glory for men will be thine appearance and thy glory for the sons of me) so many nations will express admiration at him; and kings will shut their mouths, because they, to whom no publication was made concerning him, shall see; and they who had not heard, will understand." Isa. 52:13-15

"**O Lord** who has believed this report of ours, and to whom has the arm of **the Lord** been made manifest? We have made proclamation as a child before Him, as a root in a thirsty soil; He has no appearance nor glory. We have seen him, and he has neither appearance nor beauty, but this appearance is mean and defective beyond the sons of men. Being a man in affliction and acquainted with grief, because his countenance was dejected, he was despised and disesteemed. This man beareth away our sins, and for us he is in sorrow; And we considered him as being in trouble and under a stroke and in affliction. But he was wounded for our sins, and afflicted for our iniquities. The chastisement of our peace was upon him; by his bruises we are healed. We all like sheep had strayed; every man wandered in his way: and the Lord delivered him up for our sins, and he on account of his affliction, opened not his mouth. He was led as a sheep to be slaughtered. And as a lamb before its shearers is dumb, so he opened not his mouth. In this humiliation his legal trial was taken away. Who will declare his manner of life?" Isa. 53:1-8

"Because his life is taken from the earth – for the transgressions of my people he is led to death; therefore for his funeral I will give up the wicked, and the rich for his death. Because he committed no iniquity, nor practiced guile with his mouth, and the Lord determineth to purify him from this stroke; when his should shall be given up for a sin offering, of you he shall see a seed which shall prolong their days. Moreover it is the determination of the Lord to remove him from the trouble of his soul – **to show him light and fashion him for knowledge** – to justify the Righteous One who is serving many well, when he shall bear away their sins; therefore he shall inherit many and divide the spoils of the strong." Isa. 53:9-12a

"Because his soul was delivered up to death and he was numbered among transgressors and bore the sins of many and on the account of their iniquities was delivered up;" Isa. 53:12b

****

Isaiah 53 – Bibliography "Introduction"

Let me begin by saying this book started in the 70's, when I was first saved and started hearing godly preaching on prophecy, and especially the book of Isaiah. Then I started taking notes as a police officer, Sunday School teacher and then a student at Moody Bible Institute and Lancaster Bible College, and my notebook kept growing larger.

I began to teach and preach prophecy and Isaiah, especially Isaiah 53. I went into the Pastorate and Evangelism for 18-20 years, and then entered Jewish Missions around 1994, continuing for over 30 years. I began teaching 'Hebrew-Christian Fellowships' in homes, and taught and wrote lessons on "Isaiah 53, the Crown Jewel of the Older Testament."

I taught it, re-wrote it at least ten times, and was asked by several people to publish a book on it. So, finally I sat down and put 50 years of teaching, writing, studying, gleaning and listening to prophetic teachers into a manuscript. If you find yourself in my book or on one of the pages, "to God be the glory." You have made a great and lasting impression on my life, ministry and writings. I now have about 14,000 volumes in my personal library, so you are on my shelf somewhere looking at me as I write this and talking to me as I study the Scriptures for God's glory.

I have not tried to steal any of your thoughts or teaching, I have just tried to pass them on to future generations for God's great glory. I take no credit for one jot or tittle of any volume God ever allows me to write for His glory. All the praise goes to Him and to you!

Thank You, Jesus, for dying for me on Calvary, giving me and my family eternal life, and calling me into the ministry of Your Word! This book and every book you give me the ability to write and publish is dedicated to You and to Your great glory!

Your Servant Forever,

Rev. Roger T. Boguski, Sr.

Isaiah 53 – Bibliography "Index"

1. Alexander, Joseph Addison, Dr. "The Prophecies of Isaiah" (482 pages) pp. 283-309. Zondervan Pub. House, Grand Rapids, MI. 1971. *(His preface is astounding! Dr. Hodge said, "This is his crowning labor!" Get it; Read it; Study it!)*

2. Baron, David, Founder & Director of H.C.T.I. "The Servant of JeHoVaH" 158 pages on Isaiah 53. Zondervan Pub. House, Grand Rapids, MI. 1954. *(Every believer should have a copy of this book and read it.)*

3. Barnes, Albert "Barnes' Notes – Isaiah" Vol. 2 pp. 254-287. Baker Book House 1985 + Blackie & Sons, London, 1851. *(Very Good!)*

4. Buksbazen, Victor – Th.D. "The Prophet Isaiah" pp. 400-423. The Spearhead Press, Collingswood, NJ 08107. *(Excellent!)*

5. Chambers, Oswald, "My Utmost for His Highest," various entries. Alden Press, Oxford, Great Britain 1927. *(Wonderful!)*

6. Clarke, Adam, L.L.D., F.S.A. Vol. #4 pp. 201-207. Abingdon – Cookesbury Press – N.Y. 1869. *(Very Good!)*

7. Durham, James, Rev. (Prof. of Div. of the Univ. in Glasgow). "The Marrow of the Gospel" set forth in 72 sermons – in 427 pages. Still Waters Revival Books, pub. 1723. *(Very deep and very good.)*

8. Ellicott, Charles, John (Herbert Lockyer) "Ellicott's Comm. On the Whole Bible" Vol. 4 pp. 548-551. Zondervan, Publishing House, Grand Rapids, MI. 1954. *(Very Good!)*

9. Erdman, Charles, R. Dr. "The Book of Isaiah" pp. 124-129 – Fleming H. Revell Co. 1954. *(Brief and fair.)*

10. Gill, John, D.D. Exposition of Old & New Testament – Vol. # 5 pp. 309 – 317. Reprinted by – Baptist Standard Bearer, Inc. #1 Iron Oaks Dr. Paris, AR 72855. *(Good!)*

11. Green, James, Leo, D.D. "God Reigns" – "Studies in Isaiah" Chapter 14 – pp 147 -158, Broadman Press, Nashville, TN. 1968. *(Great Study!)*

12. Grogan, Geoffrey, W. "Expositor's Bible Comm." – Vol. # 6 pp 301 – 307, Zondervan, Grand Rapids, MI 49530. *(Very Good!)*

13. Hastings, J. D.D. "The Great Texts of The Bible" Isaiah pp. 277 – 347. Charles Scribner's Son's – N.Y. 1910. *(Very Interesting Comm.)*

14. Jamieson, Robert & Fausset, A. R. & Brown, David, "A Commentary on the Old & New Testaments" Vol. #2 pp 728 – 733. Wm. B. Eerdmans Pub. Co. Grand Rapids, MI 1984. *(Very Good!)*

15. Jennings, F.C. – "Studies in Isaiah" pp 609 – 633. Loizeaux Brothers, Inc. NY 1950. *(Fair)*

16. Keil, C.F. & Delitzsch, F. (Trans. From German) Commentary of the O.T. Vol. # 7 pp 301 – 342. *(Wow! Well worth your reading! Excellent!)*

17. Lange, John Peter, D.D. (Translated from German & Edited by Philip Schaff, D.D.) "Lange's Comm. On the Holy Scriptures" – Vol. 6 pp 567 -586. Zondervan Publishing House – Grand Rapids, MI 49506. Published 1978. *(Very Good!)*

18. Leupold, J.C. "Exposition of Isaiah" Vol. 11 pp 223 -235. Baker Book House, Grand Rapids, MI 1971. *(Excellent!)*

19. MacArthur, John, Dr. "The Gospel According to God" Crossway Publishing, Wheaton, IL 60187. Published 2018. *(Buy it – Read it – Meditate on it! It is amazing! All 208 pages!)*

20. MacRae, Allan, A., Dr. "The Gospel of Isaiah" pp 129 – 150. Moody Press, Chicago, IL. Published 1956. *(Very Good!)*

21. Martin, Alfred, Th.D. "Isaiah – The Salvation of JEHOVAH." pp 89 -100. Moody Press, Chicago, IL 1956. *(Very Good!)*

22. Motyer, J. Alec, "The Prophecy of Isaiah." pp 424 – 443. Intervarsity Press, Downers Grove, IL 1993. *(Excellent!)*

23. Oswalt, John S. "NIV Application Comm. - Isaiah" pp 583 – 587. Zondervan – Grand Rapids, MI 49530. *(Very Good!)*

24. Ross, Rice, E. MA., M.Th., Ph.D. "Beacon Bible Comm." Vol. 4 pp 219 – 228. Beacon Hill Press, Kansas City, MO 1966.

25. "Scofield Study Bible," KJV – 1967, Edition/2003. E. Schuyler English, Litt.D. – Charman. *(Excellent!)*

26. Simpson, A.B. "Christ in the Bible Comm." Vol. 3, Chapter 21 pp 439 – 445. Christian Pub., Inc. Camp Hill, PA 17011. *(Reading Simpson's comm. makes you want to cry. I could have just reprinted it and let it go! However, God said, "No.")*

27. Smith, Gary, V. "New American Comm." Vol. 15b Isaiah 40-66 pp 429 – 472. B&H Publishing, Nashville, TN 2009. *(Very Good!)*

28. Sorenson, David, H.B.A., M.D.V., D. Min. "Understanding the Bible." (Prov. – Isa.) pp 635 – 646. NorthStar Ministries Publishing, Duluth, MN 55811. Published 2008. *(Fair to good.)*

29. "The Spurgeon Study Bible" KJV with Spurgeon's extensive notes pp 774 – 775. Holman Publishing, Nashville, TN 2018. *(Read verses 1 – 12 with his notes. Very Good!)*

30. Strong, James, LL.D. S.T.D. "Strong's Exhaustive Concordance of the Bible" John R. Kahlenberber III; James A. Swanson. Zondervan, Grand Rapids Publishing, MI 49350. *(Excellent!)*

31. Vine, W.E. M.A. "Vine's Expository Comm. on Isaiah" pp 145 – 152. Thomas, Nelson Pub., Nashville, TN 1997. *(Very Good. Well Done!)*

32. Watts, John, D.W. "Word Biblical Comm." Vol. 25 pp 219 – 233. Word Books, Publisher, Waco, Texas 1987. *(Very Good!)*

33. Wiersbe, Warren, W. "Bible Exposition Comm; O.T. Prophets, 'Isa. – Mal.' pp 59 – 62. 'Chapter Eleven.' Cook Communications Ministries, Colorado Springs, CO 80918. *(Very Good!)*

34. Willmington, H.L., Dr. "Willmington's Guide to the Bible, (Various Entries). Tyndale House Publishers, Inc. Wheaton, IL copyright 1981. *(Excellent!)*

35. Young, E.J. "The Book of Isaiah" Vol III pp 334 – 359. William B. Erdman's Publishing Co., Grand Rapids, MI. *(Very Good!)*

www.ingramcontent.com/pod-product-compliance
Lightning Source LLC
Chambersburg PA
CBHW030527080526
44586CB00011B/342